Dimensions of International Higher Education

Westview Special Studies

The concept of Westview Special Studies is a response to the continuing crisis in academic and informational publishing. Library budgets are being diverted from the purchase of books and used for data banks, computers, micromedia, and other methods of information retrieval. Interlibrary loan structures further reduce the edition sizes required to satisfy the needs of the scholarly community. Economic pressures on university presses and the few private scholarly publishing companies have greatly limited the capacity of the industry to properly serve the academic and research communities. As a result, many manuscripts dealing with important subjects, often representing the highest level of scholarship, are no longer economically viable publishing projects—or, if accepted for publication, are typically subject to lead times ranging from one to three years.

Westview Special Studies are our practical solution to the problem. As always, the selection criteria include the importance of the subject, the work's contribution to scholarship, and its insight, originality of thought, and excellence of exposition. We accept manuscripts in camera-ready form, typed, set, or word processed according to specifications laid out in our comprehensive manual, which contains straightforward instructions and sample pages. The responsibility for editing and proofreading lies with the author or sponsoring institution, but our editorial staff is always available to answer questions and provide guidance.

The result is a book printed on acid-free paper and bound in sturdy library-quality soft covers. We manufacture these books ourselves using equipment that does not require a lengthy make-ready process and that allows us to publish first editions of 300 to 1000 copies and to reprint even smaller quantities as needed. Thus, we can produce Special Studies quickly and can keep even very specialized books in print as long as there is a demand for them.

About the Book and Editors

The dynamics of academic exchange are explored by a multidisciplinary group of scholars in this book. Contributors from ten countries examine such issues as undergraduate versus graduate study abroad and the purpose and effect of sending students to foreign countries. Drawing on their experiences as administrators and faculty in exchange programs, the authors discuss faculty exchange, collaborative research, and linkages across national boundaries. The relative advantages of academic exchange in different fields are examined, and cross-cultural perspectives from Asia, Europe, the Middle East, and Africa are compared. The consensus of the contributors is that universities are a vital means of breaking down the barriers of nationalism by promoting a constant and free exchange of scholarship.

William H. Allaway is the Director of the University of California Education Abroad Program. **Hallam C. Shorrock** is an Associate Director of the Education Abroad Program and Adjunct Lecturer in Germanic, Oriental, and Slavic Languages and Literature at the University of California, Santa Barbara.

Published in cooperation with the Education Abroad Program,
University of California

Dimensions of International Higher Education

The University of California Symposium on Education Abroad

edited by
William H. Allaway
and Hallam C. Shorrock

Westview Press / Boulder and London

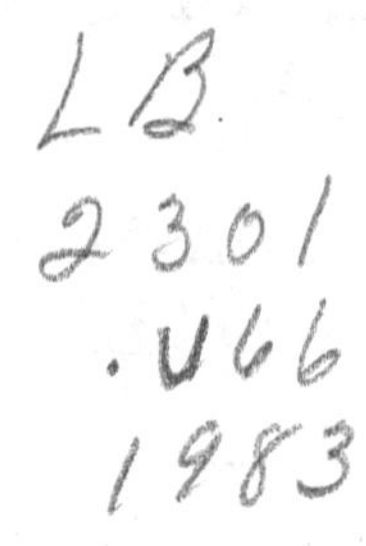

Westview Special Studies in Education

Published in 1985 in the United States by Westview Press, Inc.; Frederick A. Praeger, Publisher; 5500 Central Avenue, Boulder, Colorado 80301

Library of Congress Cataloging in Publication Data
University of California Symposium on Education
Abroad (1983: University of California, Santa
Barbara) Dimensions of international higher education.
(Westview special studies in education)
Includes index.
1. Universities and colleges—Congresses.
2. University cooperation—Congresses. 3. Educational exchange—Congresses. 4. Universities and colleges—Graduate work—Congresses. 5. Comparative education—Congresses. I. Allaway, William A. II. Shorrock, Hallam C. III. Title. IV. Series.
LB2301.U66 1983 378 85-17936
ISBN: 0-8133-7083-3

Composition for this book was provided by the editors
Printed and bound in the United States of America

10 9 8 7 6 5 4 3 2 1

This book is dedicated to the twelve thousand University of California students who have studied in more than twenty-five countries in Europe, Asia, Africa, the Middle East, Latin America, and Australia since the University of California Education Abroad Program's first study center was opened at Bordeaux in 1962; to Clark Kerr, President of the University, Emeritus, who had the vision to make it all possible; and to the three UC Santa Barbara Chancellors who have provided their dedicated support: Samuel B. Gould, Vernon I. Cheadle, and Robert A. Huttenback.

Contents

PART THREE
ACADEMIC AND CULTURAL DIMENSIONS OF STUDY ABROAD

Foreword

Clark W. Kerr

Public concern for international affairs has never been a consistently high priority in the United States. Historically, attention has gone instead to populating and developing a new nation, isolated from the religious and political quarrels of the older nation-states. American higher education, on the other hand, has always had at least some international dimensions. The founding of colleges in the American colonies relied heavily on European sources for funds and academic leadership. Through the nineteenth century migration of graduate students to German universities and the adoption of aspects of the German research university by American institutions and into the construction of a twentieth-century international community of scholars, especially in scientific fields, higher education in the United States has been international. There has always been some very considerable exchange of knowledge, of ideas, of people.

Only since World War II, however, has that international aspect been a self-conscious one on the part of institutions of higher education and of public policy, and the forms that interest and policy have taken have closely followed the bends and turns of international relations. In the 1940s, plans for postwar reconstruction of Europe and Japan included proposals to rebuild and restaff educational institutions at all levels to provide a basis for a stable international order. The Fulbright Program of intellectual cooperation paralleled the Marshall Plan of economic cooperation and development.

Through the 1950s, Cold War and national defense needs stimulated the development of area studies and foreign language centers. During the early 1960s, interest turned to supplying technical assistance to developing nations of the world and to their institutions of newly acquired university status, as in Nigeria, Ghana, and East Africa.

In the later 1960s and 1970s, however, increasing international trade and investment by Americans abroad, the emergence of multinational companies as a "sixth continent" (as Sir Kenneth Alexander notes in his presentation in Chapter 10), and heavy traffic by travelers and vacationers across national boundaries were not accompanied by parallel increases in national support for the international aspects of higher education. The effects of the Vietnam War on the United States included a public disenchantment with international involvements and, on university campuses, one side effect of the civil and academic turbulence was a loosening of curricular requirements, especially in foreign languages and humanities, areas that served to underpin international education. At the same time, the massive injection of Ford Foundation funds that had done so much to stimulate foreign area studies ceased, as that organization turned to other, more domestic, problems. As a result, by the late 1970s support for international education activities such as teacher exchanges, area study centers, and NDEA fellowships had dropped dramatically.

Since the late 1970s, the theme of a "global perspective" has emerged, and that theme is expressed throughout this volume. The notion of a "global village" has replaced the older international dream of a "world order," and emphasizes the interdependence of all the peoples of the world. Economically, we can no longer speak of a "First" or "Second" or "Third World" when, as Peter Drucker has pointed out, "production sharing" -- the participation of workers and capital in several countries in the making of a single object, such as a pair of shoes -- is rapidly replacing even multinational corporations as the preferred form of economic integration.[1] There is a new recognition, too, of the ways in which all are dependent on the same ecosphere, and of the fact that the threat of nuclear war is a threat of global destruction. The question is, in what ways will higher education respond to a world that David Saxon describes, in the closing chapter, as "technological, xenophobic, and nuclear"?

While, as indicated above, Americans have retreated from a national commitment to programs of international education, individual students have continued to cross national boundaries in search of broad educational and cultural experiences. The number of foreign students in the United States grew from 50,000 in 1960-1961 to over 300,000 in 1983-1984, and by the late 1970s foreign students for the first time constituted over 2 percent of all higher education enrollments in the United States. As enrollment rates have flattened, that percentage continues to increase, and in 1983-84 foreign students made up nearly 3 percent of total enrollments in American colleges and universities.

As the demographic decline in the traditional college-going age cohort steepens in the next few years, higher education institutions all over the United States will continue their efforts to fill classrooms and dormitories with qualified students. If college enrollment drops at the same 20 percent rate as the age cohort will decline in the next twenty years, there will be a surplus of about 2.4 million places as compared with the some 12 million enrolled in 1980. That is over seven times the number of foreign students now enrolled in United States higher education institutions, and at least some of those available places might be filled by students from abroad. They will be most likely to come from countries, such as China, that now have very low rates of participation and in which expansion of existing systems of higher education demands a very large portion of resources that are also needed for economic development.

Not only students, but many individual institutions have sustained a commitment to international education in all its facets, even as national trends have succumbed to vacillations in national moods and policies. The symposium, held in conjunction with the

20th anniversary of the founding of the University of California's Education Abroad Program (and with the University's 115th birthday), the occasion of these presentations, demonstrates the longstanding commitment of this institution to international education.

The range of themes touched upon in the symposium papers is impressive. First, in keeping with the marking of the anniversary of the Education Abroad Program, is the emphasis on student exchanges, especially at the undergraduate level. The papers explore the academic, the personal, and the broader cultural aspects of the experience of living and learning in a nation and culture other than one's own, pointing to the problems and dangers as well as to the benefits. Eleven of the American participants in the symposium have had experience as administrators in a University of California Education Abroad center, and they underscore the importance of support mechanisms for undergraduate students if only, as Neil Smelser describes it (Ed. note: Chapter 6), to provide information on how to make a hairdryer work on a different voltage! Ørjar Øyen's paper (Ed. note: Chapter 7) is particularly instructive on the often neglected question of how the ambiguous goals we have for international student exchanges are actually translated into cross-cultural influences by the participating students themselves. His discussion of the "marginals" and the "centrals" in any society, the former having weak ties to any one group and therefore being more open to new influences which they then diffuse to the more ethnocentric members of the society, brings social science theory to bear on the processes by which cultural change takes place.

A second major theme of the symposium relates to the academic or knowledge aspect of international education. The set of papers dealing with challenges and opportunities for international exploration in different disciplinary areas and in different parts of the world raises questions about the ways in which methodologies and technologies are embedded in cultures, and are also conditioned by social and economic contexts. For example, in those fields where curricular requirements are sequential, tightly controlled, and oriented to specific job markets, as in engineering and some scientific fields, the knowledge base, and even the community of scholars, may be highly internationalized, but exchanges of students minimal, as several authors pointed out. Students in these fields may not be able to transfer the methodologies practiced in one nation into a base for subsequent work in the home country, and may not be able to receive academic credit for work that is perceived to be outside the normal progression toward a degree. In the humanities, on the other hand, the subject matter may be quite different from what is taught in the home institution, but the cultural and linguistic milieu may well provide the greatest benefit of the international experience. Credit may also be granted for work in non-sequential courses.

A third overarching theme of the symposium papers deals with the institutional arrangements that support international education in all its forms. Arrangements that are explored here include collaborative research teams drawing membership from several countries (an especially useful device for smaller nations), faculty exchanges, and formal academic linkages between universities which then share a variety of resources. Of special interest is Elwin V. Svenson's discussion (Ed. note: Chapter 9) of the ties between the University of California and the University of Chile. His paper explores the often delicate relationships and decisions that are necessary when one of the participating academic institutions is located in a country with a repressive political regime.

As Barbara Burn so positively affirms (Ed. note: Chapter 4), higher education is international, and its institutions must continue to develop a wide variety of means, many of which are described in this volume, which will allow not only international education, but the internationalization of education, to permeate our colleges and universities.

I should like to take this opportunity to note that neither this symposium nor the study abroad program which it celebrates would have been possible without the devoted efforts of William H. Allaway. He has contributed such excellent judgment, such formidable efforts, and such constant patience and goodwill for so many years to the Education Abroad Program of which the University of California is so justly proud and from which so many thousands of students have so greatly benefitted. I have seen him at work since the earliest days of this Program when I participated in its establishment, and have always thought that the Program was in the best of all possible hands.

NOTES

1. Peter F. Drucker, Managing in Turbulent Times (New York: Harper and Row, 1980), p. 96.

Preface

The essays and commentaries which form the content of this book were originally presented on April 14 and 15, 1983, on the occasion of the 115th anniversary of the chartering of the University of California (UC) and the 20th anniversary of the establishment of the University's Education Abroad Program (EAP). Following the anniversary celebrations, a one-day Symposium on International Education, sponsored by the Education Abroad Program, took place on the UC Santa Barbara campus. The symposium brought together nearly 200 persons. Participants included leading faculty and administrators in international higher education in the United States and from nine countries where the University of California maintains reciprocal exchange agreements with other universities, past and present regents, EAP participants and staff members.

The symposium, which provided the occasion for the presentation and sharing of these papers and the interchange among participants, celebrated twenty years of unusual cooperation between the University of California and distinguished universities around the world. Through the sharing of common objectives and of resources, the education of many thousands of students has been enriched through a period of study in a university in another country. Faculty members have had a unique experience assisting students in maximizing that experience while furthering their own scholarly objectives.

The contents of this volume provide ample evidence of the complexity of educational exchange in its motivations, its conceptualization, and its implementation. The joys, the anguish, and the mind-bending nature of the experience for students are analyzed and celebrated. Indeed, the student is given a uniquely central role in thrusting into the forefront the major mission of the university, that of purveying scholarship to succeeding generations. The beauty of it all is that while individual scholars of all ages have had these transforming experiences, the universities concerned have gone calmly about their business, because what was occurring was what has come naturally to universities ever since the institutionalization of higher education began to take place.

True, scholarly communication occurs in many languages from Sanskrit to FORTRAN. True, faculty committees can debate endlessly the number of units a student from UC Berkeley should receive for a seminar taken in the ancient University of Padua. True, a junior faculty member from the University of Nairobi who takes a Ph.D. at UC Davis can bring new insights in his chosen field to further his teaching and research in Kenya. True, students will say that regardless of their academic progress in degree terms at the University of California, the year abroad remains the major educational experience of their lifetime. These statements only hint at the complexities of the subject under discussion.

During the past twenty years, the interchange of students and faculty across national borders has steadily increased. In addition to the more than fifty universities in more than twenty-five countries with which the University of California is linked through exchanges, by means of this volume may I salute universities and countries everywhere which throw open their doors to share their uniqueness with friends and colleagues of another nation, another culture, and often another language. At the same time I wish to express a final word of deep appreciation to colleagues throughout the University of California system who have done so much to make the EAP what it is today and who shared their experiences with us in the symposium, and particularly to my colleagues in the EAP who have demonstrated so amply that a bureaucracy can be a caring community with a mission. Special thanks must go to co-editor Hallam C. Shorrock without whose efforts this volume would never have seen the light of day.

It is our sincere hope that the sharing of the material will contribute to the internationalization -- the globalization -- of higher education, not only for the sake of its enrichment, but, as then UC President David Saxon so eloquently stated, as "a necessity for survival in our nuclear world."

William H. Allaway, Director
University of California
Education Abroad Program

Acknowledgments

In addition to each of the contributors who are named in the following section, faculty colleagues who chaired the symposium plenary sessions and discussion groups, and who were discussion leaders and rapporteurs (see Appendix for the University of California 115th Anniversary and EAP Symposium Program), the editors wish to acknowledge the staff persons who assisted in the recording of the presentations, the editing and word processing of the texts, and in the logistical arrangements for the symposium.

Administrative and secretarial work: Karen Kisselburgh Ahmadizadeh and Ann Heyada Nomura.

Financial arrangements and logistics: Gloria D. Blakemore, Patricia A. Chackel, and Ann D. Sorg.

Public address and recording systems: UCSB media equipment scheduler Liz Schoofs and her student staff.

Editorial assistance: Eric Beck-Jensen, Michelle Lettington Bobro, Valerie Swanson, and Henry D. Weaver.

Word processing: Sarah Duvall and DiAnna Joiner.

Camera-ready copy: Michelle Lettington Bobro.

About the Contributors

Sir Kenneth Alexander is Principal and Vice Chancellor, University of Stirling, Scotland.

William H. Allaway is the Director of the University of California Education Abroad Program.

William M. Brinner is Professor of Near Eastern Studies, UC Berkeley, was Director of the Education Abroad Program Study Center in Israel from 1973 to 1975, and served as the 1984-1985 Chairman of the University Committee of the Education Abroad Program.

Barbara B. Burn is Director of International Programs, University of Massachusetts at Amherst.

Louise George Clubb is Professor of Italian and Comparative Literature, UC Berkeley and was Director of the Education Abroad Program Study Center at the University of Padua from 1980 to 1982. She recently accepted an appointment as Director of Harvard's Center for Italian Renaissance Studies in Florence, Italy.

James S. Coleman was, until his death in April 1985, Professor of Political Science and Director of International Studies and Overseas Programs, UC Los Angeles.

Ralf Dahrendorf is Professor of Social Science at the University of Konstanz, West Germany; he was formerly Director of the London School of Economics and Political Science.

Jorge Fontana is Professor of Electrical Engineering and was formerly Deputy Director of the Education Abroad Program.

Naftaly S. Glasman is Professor of Education and Political Science, and Dean of the Graduate School of Education, UC Santa Barbara.

Ampah Johnson is Professor and Rector of the University of Benin, Lome, Togo, and President of the Africa Club.

Joyce K. Kallgren is Professor of Political Science, UC Davis, and the Chair of the Center for Chinese Studies, UC Berkeley.

Norbert Kamp is Professor of Medieval History and since 1979 has been President of Georg-August University, Goettingen.

Dmitri Georges Lavroff is the President of the University of Law, Economics, Science and Technology of Bordeaux, and past President of the Liaison Committee of the Conferences of University Chancellors of the Member Countries of the European Communities.

Choh-Ming Li is the founding Vice Chancellor (President) of The Chinese University of Hong Kong and Professor Emeritus of Business Administration, UC Berkeley.

John A. Marcum is Professor of Politics and former Academic Vice Chancellor, UC Santa Cruz.

Dennis C. McElrath is Professor of Sociology, Stevenson College, UC Santa Cruz, and was Director of the Education Abroad Program Study Center at the University of Padua from 1974 to 1976.

Ørjar Øyen is Professor of Sociology and at the time of the symposium was the Rector of the University of Bergen, Norway.

S.B. Saul is Professor and Vice Chancellor, University of York.

David S. Saxon was the President of the University of California from July 1, 1975 to June 30, 1983 when he became Chairman of the Corporation of the Massachusetts Institute of Technology.

Hallam C. Shorrock is an Associate Director of the Education Abroad Program and Adjunct Lecturer, Germanic, Oriental and Slavic Languages and Literatures, UC Santa Barbara.

Neil J. Smelser is University Professor of Sociology, UC Berkeley; he was Director of the Education Abroad Program Study Center in the United Kingdom and Ireland from 1977 to 1979.

R.J. Snow was Vice President for University Relations, University of Utah, at the time of the Symposium. He was Associate Director of the Education Abroad Program Study Center at Bordeaux from 1971 to 1973.

Manfred Stassen is Director of the German Academic Exchange Service in New York (Deutscher Akademischer Austauschdienst) and Vice President of the International Society for Educational, Cultural and Scientific Exchanges.

Nils N. Stjernquist is Professor of Political Science and at the time of the symposium was the Vice Chancellor of the University of Lund, Sweden.

Elwin V. Svenson is Vice Chancellor-Institutional Relations, UC Los Angeles.

Yoash Vaadia is Professor of Plant Physiology and Vice President, Finance and Administration, of The Hebrew University of Jerusalem.

Part One

The International Environment

1
To Be an Educated Person in a Technological Society

David S. Saxon

In many ways 1962, the year the University of California Education Abroad Program began, seems a remote and distant time and place, far less complex, less forbidding, than our own day. But in one way, at least, the world has not changed. We still need the contributions that only educated people can make. And yet when we examine what we mean when we speak of an educated person in today's world, it seems to me that we confront a deep unanswered question, a question that is -- more often than not -- inadequately formulated and insufficiently addressed. The challenge for both European and American education is this: How do we give our students the kind of education that will prepare them not merely for some particular career but for a future of unknown and unknowable possibilities? How, in short, do we give them a genuinely liberal education?

There are two dimensions to that challenge. The first is the profound need to educate ourselves for life in our increasingly and irreversibly technological society. Science and technology have wrought so many changes in the way we live and in the way we perceive the world that no educated person can afford to be ignorant of the character and limits of science, and no person ignorant of the character and limits of science can be called educated. One of the distinguishing marks of a liberal education is the ability to winnow out the meretricious from the meritorious, to distinguish sense from nonsense. And yet many educated people are unable to do anything of the sort when it comes to questions connected in almost any way with science and technology. In the United States, and no doubt the same is true, to one degree or another, just about everywhere, we have a long way to go before our citizenry receives the kind of grounding in science that it needs to make the decisions thrust upon us by life in this complicated technological world.

One of the barriers to the kind of understanding I have talked about is the difficulty of acquiring the tools of quantitative thinking, especially mathematics. We need to do a better job of encouraging students to prepare themselves for the study of science by learning such skills early on in their education. This will never happen unless students, and their mentors, are convinced that an understanding of science is as much a part of a liberal education as the study of history or philosophy or literature.

But besides an understanding of science, anyone who aspires to be educated in today's world must be thoroughly familiar with, and must understand other countries and other cultures. And just as a lack of quantitative skills hampers the study of science, so inadequate linguistic training frustrates the effort to learn about other cultures. The failure of American education to give its students a firm grounding in foreign languages is an old deficiency that verges on a national scandal. That failure makes the achievements of programs like Education Abroad all the more impressive, of course. But we will never really address the problem until we begin to look at it with the seriousness it deserves, until we begin the study of language not with high school or college but with the beginning of education itself.

What I have been arguing is that to be an educated person today requires, among other things, a knowledge of two kinds of reality: the reality of the physical world of nature and the human world of culture. Technology has brought all of us closer together through the worldwide communications network it has created, which makes it impossible for us to ignore each other even if we wanted to. But rapid communication does not guarantee understanding, and it is one of the permanently valuable contributions of the Education Abroad Program that it seeks to foster both intelligent exchange and the understanding that goes along with a genuine effort to see the world from another culture's point of view. Just as it makes no sense for scientists and humanists to perpetuate the idea and reality of two separate cultures, unable to understand or communicate with each other, so it makes no sense in today's world for peoples of different countries and cultures to spend their lives in a state of mutual incomprehension. International understanding is not simply a polite idea; it is a necessity for survival in our nuclear world.

2
The Danger of Academic Protectionism

Ralf Dahrendorf

I hesitate to describe my first visit to this country as an example of "education abroad." In the early months of 1951, I was a student at the University of Hamburg, and had just begun my doctoral dissertation when the opportunity was offered to me to travel as a mess steward on a German cargo vessel from Antwerp to New York, on to Cuba, and back to Bremerhaven. We carried scrap iron to New York. In the rough seas of the North Atlantic, our 4,500 ton ship seemed as if it had itself been found on a scrap heap to form a part of the infant post-war German merchant navy. Then, there were my books, suspicious books at the time: for example, my dissertation on Karl Marx, and this was the McCarthy period. However, nobody suspected anything at Bethlehem Steel's pier in Hoboken. New York was, at the time, a slow port, without cranes; the mess steward had a week to himself. After the first evening, which I spent with my fellow sailors in Yorkville, in places called Mozart Hall or Rheingold Bar, I ventured further afield. I went to Columbia University, where the officer responsible for foreign students, a woman who was training to be a teacher, took me and three others in a ramshackle car to her hometown in upstate New York. She stopped at the petrol station, and the owner invited one of us to his home; she stopped at the general store, and off went another one of us. I spent two memorable days in the home of a local craftsman. He took me to church, where I was greeted as a friend from far away, never mind my not being a member. He took me to neighbors who asked many questions and listened intently to what I had to tell.

Education abroad? Perhaps not. But I left with a deep sense of the openness, the human generosity, to say nothing of the hospitality and directness of the Americans whom I had met. I left with a sense of gratitude, and of difference. It may not have changed my own ways, but it did implant in me the memory of another culture, and thus of questions about my own culture which would have remained unasked otherwise. It made me a more critical and thus, I believe, a more aware, a richer human being.

My own institution, the London School of Economics and Political Science, or LSE for short, has been international from its beginnings in 1895. Since the 1930s, more than one-third of our students have come from abroad. Some became, admittedly, uncomfortable friends of Britain, the founders of new nations, like

Jomo Kenyatta of Kenya, or leading radical politicians, like Krishna Menon of India. Others became leaders of developed countries, like Queen Margaretha of Denmark, or Pierre Trudeau of Canada. We pride ourselves on having not only twenty-nine British members of Parliament, but also, for example, two U.S. senators. One of them, Senator Patrick Moynihan of New York, is the president of our American Friends. I do not say this as a commercial for the LSE, proud though I am of it; I say it in order to underline the point that it is the best who have been abroad, exposed to different ways, forced to ask questions about themselves which might otherwise have gone unasked, richer -- as public servants, but also as private persons -- for the experience, and altogether aware of wider horizons.

The problem is that today it must be said, and said again, that this is not a time of internationalism. Ever since the golden decades of economic growth, of expanding trade, transnational economic activity, and rising welfare came to an end in the 1970s, there has been a growing tendency to look inward. This has affected education; further than that, it has affected trade, and in the end affected the very texture of cooperation on which the international community is built.

To some extent, the reasons are evident. Declining growth, coupled with the promises built into civilized states, has meant pressure on public expenditure, even if the process was not coupled with new promises in the field of defense. If public expenditure is cut, the weakest take the cut first. For some reason, education is among the weakest. A former British Secretary of State for Education once said to me: "Universities can't win: Conservatives believe that all lecturers are radicals; the Labour Party believes that all students are middle-class children and the coalition of the two is unbeatable." Whatever truth there may be to this, and whatever analogous reasons there may be in less class-conscious countries, education abroad has certainly suffered. We in Britain have seen the fees for overseas students go up from 250 to 3,000 pounds and more in a period of ten years. At the same time, little money has been available for British students to go overseas. It was only when this policy began to have tangible repercussions on trade, with Southeast Asia for example, that the government introduced certain minor changes.

In any case, the less tangible reasons are the more important. We are living in a climate which is increasingly hostile to internationalism. Understandably perhaps, if domestic industries are in trouble, people wonder why the same products should be imported from elsewhere. Why have textiles from Taiwan, steel from Korea, cars from Japan, agricultural products from Europe, if one can produce these things oneself? The demand for protection grows. It has always been strong in this country with its enormous internal market and relatively low dependence on exports. But it is growing elsewhere, including in the export-intensive countries of the European Community, and it is getting worse in the United States. There is a kind of creeping protectionism, often indirect, not necessarily in direct contravention of any article of the General Agreement on Tariffs and Trade.

Now you may ask: what is wrong with it? The answer has more general application. However large the internal market may be, protection sets in motion a spiral of stagnation and impoverishment. If one's industries are no longer exposed to the winds of international competition, they do not have to adapt to new demands, technological or otherwise. If they do not adapt, they produce more slowly; indeed, there is no incentive to prevent them from deteriorating in quality and lagging in quantity. In the end, behind the tariff walls, people will begin to queue as they do in Eastern Europe. They will wait a year for a car, six months for a television set, and when they get them, the products will break down and it will be difficult to have them repaired. Turning away from the world means foregoing one's chances of growth and improvement.

But, of course, grasping these chances presupposes self-confidence. Protectionism is the way of fearful, frightened people. When I was responsible for foreign trade and foreign policy as a member of the Commission of the European Community, it always made me suspicious when employers and trade unions of a particular industry came and displayed total agreement. It usually meant that they were afraid and wanted protection. This was the case of the European textile industry; agriculture everywhere having gone down the road of protectionism a long time ago. Today, self-confidence is hard to come by. Many fearful events surround us. The persistent economic recession and its effects on social services and on employment provide but one example. In this country, as in the rest of the world, including Eastern Europe, the fear of nuclear destruction is spreading. Thus, it has rarely been more important to educate self-confident people. To go abroad, to see others and their ways, to try and understand them, to go back with a new appreciation of oneself, is certainly one element of that self-confidence which is so badly needed.

A time of fear is also a time people remember the smaller units to which they belong: family, peer group, village. It would be wrong to detract from such preferences. In many ways, it is true: small <u>is</u> beautiful. We made terrible mistakes during the 1960s when we thought that "economies of scale" must mean that bigger is better. Today, we know that very often the right scale is the smaller scale. In business, this is by now commonplace; in the way in which we organize our communities, we still have a lot to learn. But when all is said and done, "small is beautiful" is only one side of the story; the other side is, "big is necessary." In other words, we need not only as much decentralization as possible, but also as much centralization as necessary. Centralization may mean the state, the federal government, or some international agency, the Alliance, the United Nations.

Much of what I have said applies to Europe as it does to the United States. I have stated it freely therefore, and without the reticence which a guest must always feel when he begins to give advice to his hosts. Yet, I cannot resist saying at this point that there are many of us in Europe who feel that it would be disastrous for the world if this great country, the United States of America, allowed itself to be carried away by the new mood of fear, and of looking inward. None of the three great issues before us in the world can be solved without a confident, and understanding United States of America.

The first of these issues is to maintain the conditions of prosperity all over the world. They were maintained as long as they were guaranteed by the United States; indeed, the post-war world order was a pax Americana. We in the other free countries must understand that in economic respects, at least, such one-sidedness could not continue forever. The collapse of the international monetary system in 1971 could probably not have been avoided. At the same time, there is no chance of rebuilding an international monetary system without the United States. Rudimentary beginnings like the European Monetary System are no more than that. Ultimately, the United States must play a special -- not a singular, but a special -- role in the re-building of monetary order. The same is true for trade, and for all other rules governing the international economic system.

The second major issue is even less popular. None of us here will live to see a world in which all human beings have the ability to live a civilized life. Worse, all of us here will see a world in which millions of people will die of starvation or avoidable disease. Most of us, I suppose, will try not to see it, will look away. It will happen nevertheless. These people, in South Asia, in Africa south of the Sahara, in parts of Latin America, do not need guns; they need help. It is, I believe, an irrefutable obligation of all humans to make sure that no one, but no one in our world is denied elementary citizenship rights. These include material things, food, shelter, medical care; they also include basic elements of the rule of law.

How do we go about implementing these lofty principles? You will have noticed that I have not spoken of the interdependence of North and South which will force us to help the poor. In some cases, such interdependence exists. But, in the first instance, our obligation is moral. To implement it, we need to support those who have proved successful in the past. Of the large international institutions, this includes the World Bank system; of those working in the field, it includes, above all, churches and many kinds of voluntary organizations. The more people spend their time abroad helping those in need, the more world citizens we will have. So far as human rights are concerned, we are strangely powerless. Here, the word is still the most effective weapon. We must never cease to condemn those who torture, imprison without trial, put dissidents in psychiatric hospitals, use forced labor, or do one of the many other horrible things which human beings can do to each other.

Then there is the third great issue, defense. Even more than with respect to the others, the role of the United States is special here. In the post-war world, the security of the free countries has been based first on superiority, then on that frightening stalemate called deterrence. Underneath the military force, it has been based on the alliance of the free countries, on common beliefs and on mutual trust. This Alliance (with a capital A) is as important today as it ever was. It is strong, and it must remain strong. There are few people in the free Europe who do not share this belief, which I certainly regard as the very foundation of liberty in our imperfect world.

But there are differences of view concerning the ways in which the Alliance should express its strength. These differences require a lot of mutual understanding, more perhaps than all concerned have shown in recent years. Deterrence means just that; it can never mean that a nuclear war can actually be conducted. Deterrence is indivisible; there must be no attempt to uncouple any part of the Alliance. Deterrence in the nuclear age means sufficiency; it does not mean that each side has to be precisely as strong in all respects as the other. Deterrence is a necessary expedient, not a desirable state; reducing the level of nuclear armament and beginning a downward spiral of disarmament is therefore a crucial part of security. These are some of the beliefs of those of us in Europe who cherish liberty, trust the Alliance and accept the needs of defense, but who wonder from time to time whether our motives are fully understood in Washington.

I have strayed a long way from the happy educational occasion which has brought us together. Or have I? Understanding others is one of the great human virtues. Understanding is what universities are about. "Felix qui potuit rerum cognoscere causes" ("Happy is he who can understand the causes of things"), said Virgil. The latter part of this verse, understanding the causes of things, is the motto of the London School of Economics; it could be the motto of all universities. Understanding, however, does not come about by merely delving into subjects, by attending classes, reading books and the like. Understanding requires a kind of shock of recognition. A generation ago, many young people experienced this shock by entering the halls of a university at all; they were the first in their families to do so, and to live the life of the mind for a period was not only their dream but also involved a great break. In Britain, there is a whole literature about the "scholarship boys" (and girls, of course), those who got there by public assistance and now felt unsure of both where they were going and whence they were coming. Today, universities have become so much a part of most people's lives that this particular shock is more rare. Could education abroad take its place?

In this country, universities themselves provide a home for people from diverse cultures. Indeed, the best universities have always done that. Even so, a change of context is unique as a method for providing the helpful shock of difference. If protectionism got hold of the academic world, this would not only lead to intellectual stagnation and deterioration, but would also fail those students, young and not so young, who rightly expect the fleeting years of academic freedom to provide them with new experience, with experience that makes them grow as human beings as well as lawyers, engineers, or even sociologists. Those of us who have responsibility for universities also have the responsibility for keeping their doors wide open.

Part Two

Affirming the International Character of Higher Education

3
The International Roots of Higher Education

D. G. Lavroff

"Higher Education Is International" is a fine topic, but it is difficult to resolve and even, indeed, to present. In fact, the utterance of this phrase may be taken as a question or as a proposition. In the case of a question, we can try to find an answer, thereby examining instances where the factual evidence establishes that higher education is, indeed, international and hence try to project future developments. In lending an affirmative mode to the phrase, a critical appraisal seems called for, because it is far from certain that higher education is, in reality, international. Also, the question arises as to the opportuneness of the establishment of international higher education, to be organized on lines which remain to be drawn up. It is this second conception that calls for an affirmation.

Higher education was certainly international at its outset. The very existence of higher education supposes that the community in question has succeeded in setting up a system of elementary education. This latter can take many different forms, but it must be capable of providing its alumni with a sufficient grounding. It appears, notable from the work of Plato, that ancient Greece had a system of higher education. He draws a very careful distinction between two levels in the education program, separating the subjects leading to the acquisition of applied and applicable knowledge and those tending towards the perception of truth. The former studies were for the warriors, while the dialectic was the science of the philosopher. From this point on, education was international, at least as far as its object was concerned; it was no longer a question of the dissemination of factual instruction, but of affording access to principles beyond spatial and temporal limitations.

Rome gave further evidence of an intelligent international higher education. Although there is no doubt of the superiority of their form of society, the Romans of the empire were able to get away from the narrow restraints of localism and to open themselves to varied influences. The importance of the Greek poets, philosophers, and mathematicians regarding the development of the elite of Roman society is common knowledge. Romans did not become Greeks, but they were able to enrich themselves and, in conquering the world, allow their offspring to benefit from the best in the lands they controlled.

At the birth of the first Western European universities in the early part of the thirteenth century, their teaching was clearly international. This example requires some explanation since our universities are more or less directly descended from them.

The universities of the Middle Ages are original institutions. They appeared following a sufficient development of the elementary education in accordance with the obligation of the bishops to establish schools in each diocese and monastery. The university was a community grouping masters and pupils. Between 1209 and 1215, the first universities were created at Bologna, Valencia, Oxford and Paris.

These medieval universities are notable for their universalism, at least within the context of the Christian world. It was the internationalism of teachers who hopped between Paris and Oxford or Bologna and Salamanca. The students were marked by their internationalism as well, and by their itinerant style. They went where their subjects led them, following their masters as they went. It is worth noting that although the universities had an Arts Faculty for first-year students, it was not the case that every university had faculties in all the disciplines nor teachers of equal worth. The University of Bologna had an excellent Law Faculty; Montpellier was regarded as an important center for medicine; Oxford excelled in mathematics, and Orleans was the center for grammar and poetic humanism. The teachers and pupils were spread among universities according to their prestige and their means.

The universal rather than the international character of medieval higher education was neither a chance happening nor the outcome of concerted action, but rather the result of various causes. There existed a philosophical unity in the medieval world which overlapped with Christianity. Kingdoms and principalities vied with each other, but rested on the same model, the same foundations of principle. There existed a linguistic unity, at least at the level of higher education, which was always conducted in Latin. The culture disseminated was homogenous. It was founded on the classical models of Greece and Rome, sometimes with Arabic elements interposed. Roman law provided the common base for legal instruction. Christian theology accented life and dominated philosophical reflection. The cultural homogeneity rendered higher education insensible to the national differences understood as depending on the diversity of local forms of communication. In such a world, the elite was interchangeable: a Frenchman could become a chancellor in England, a Spaniard a bishop in Germany or in France.

In the fourteenth century, however, the universalism of the universities fell into decline. The princes sought to control the universities in whose charge were their future servants. In this way, the universities of Prague, Krakow, Dole, and Louvain came into being. It was to avoid ever depending on universities outside their dominion, the civil law being then taught at Orleans, that the Duke of Bedford and Henry VI founded the Universities of Caen and Bordeaux. The questioning of the universality of Christianity, the development of national languages to the detriment of Latin, the creating of kingdoms seeking political and administrative cohesion, in time, dealt a fatal blow to the initial universalism. More and more, it led the way towards the national higher education which dominates the nineteenth and twentieth centuries.

The decline in the international character of superior higher education was the consequence of the creation of the nation-state. The cause, or the effect, of the dislocation of medieval Christianity was the founding of the nation-states. Even before this movement reached its termination during the course of the nineteenth century in Europe, the ancient kingdoms and principalities had gradually shed their ancient feudal form to become states more or less centered on monarchical power. The appearance of frontiers in the place of the ancient "marches" which divided the large territorial masses in a fairly flexible manner, marked an important turning point. The political entities henceforth grouped themselves around a single monarch, along with the contingent administrative hierarchy, the whole given a particular resonance with the adoption of a national language.

The abandonment of Latin as a language of instruction and the adoption of national languages evidently delivered a fatal blow to the international character of higher education. Students had greater and greater difficulty in attending higher education in foreign parts. In comparison, teachers had relatively greater freedom, but the careers of a large number progressed with difficulty in foreign universities.

The nationalization of higher education is the result of an increase in the number of students. International higher education has difficulty in accommodating a vast number of students. Thus, a method suitable for several hundreds or thousands of students was maladapted to the tens or hundreds of thousands of students appearing in Europe and America. Economic restrictions prevented the possibility, or even the inclination, of the students to pursue their studies in countries other than their own. The development of higher education -- which is to the good -- contradicts its international character.

It must not be overlooked that higher education has become an instrument of power and a bastion of sovereignty. It was true in the long distant past that the acquisition of culture and a high level of knowledge was a matter for the individual tending towards the cultivation of his personality. It is clear that states hold, rightly one may add, that the cultural and scientific level of the populace is an element of their strength. Thus, in judging the comparative strength and importance of a state, the level of its technological development, and the ways in which such development affects its industrial force, commercial strength, and military power, are as crucial as the size of its population. In such objective conditions as these, how can a state be expected to leave the higher education of its nationals in the hands of foreigners? How could a state accept without limitations the numbers of students arriving to study within its borders? In the former case, that would have amounted to placing in the hands of others the responsibilities of deciding its future development. In the latter case, it would be a question of bearing a heavy financial burden in an activity which could one day turn against the state. This is perhaps a cynical, but equally, a true observation.

The recent evolution of the policies of newly independent states serves to illustrate this movement. Upon obtaining independence, the new African and Asian states took stock of their economic and cultural dependence. They first realized that it was necessary to regain control of their natural resources. It was at once the most obvious and the most difficult need to satisfy. The seeking of cultural independence was of equal importance. Colonization brought about a destruction of cultural identity which was felt hard by the elite, who considered that they were losing their personalities. The governments of newly independent states were initially faced with a choice: attain a modern culture via the university system which had been established and, in turn, left behind by the colonizing power, or regain the lost cultural identity in accepting the renunciation of the international opening as offered by the now foreign universities. During the initial phase, the first alternative was adopted, to be gradually replaced by the second. A proliferation of national universities was then witnessed to supplant those left by the colonial force. They bore first an African or Asian character, then abandoned this pluri-national aspect to withdraw squarely within the frontiers of the state. While it is understandable that formerly colonized states should wish to escape from cultural domination, it is to be regretted that the nationalistic character of the new universities has prevailed over pluri-national higher education, which would have led to the development of an African or Asian identity. At the present time, underpopulated states, or those with low levels of student population, have opted for a strictly nationalistic education rather than for a grouping of several such states.

The development of national higher education is a means to defend autonomy against the domination of states enjoying technological and cultural advantages. The closing of frontiers, even with regard to foreign ideas and cultures, is an understandable temptation for weaker states. One can mock the attitude, resulting in an unfortunate isolation, but it is a reaction to the danger of disappearance which has the beneficial effect of preserving a culture in jeopardy under a temporarily dominating civilization. Even when administered in overtly nationalistic universities, higher education naturally maintains an international aspect. Science is quintessentially universal. The desire to enclose oneself within artificial barriers is, first of all, to condemn oneself to stagnation and, secondly, to regression. It is impossible to develop higher education based on purely national knowledge, experience, or discoveries. The Romans were formally enriched by the contributions of the Greeks; Christianity of the Middle Ages, albeit convinced of its exclusive possession of truth, did not refuse the offerings of the moderns. European civilization dominated the world for a time, but profited equally from the influence of black music and painting and better comprehended its own nature in examining different cultures. By contrast, cultures locked within hermetic frontiers have vegetated and regressed. The example of China is well-known, along with the evil consequences of nationalistic pride which rejects all that is foreign. In order that higher education may progress, it must become increasingly international.

The necessity of efforts for more international higher education is beyond question. To lament the passing of the ancient universities is not a serious proposition, destroyed as it was by mounting nationalism. A return to the past is neither desirable nor possible and would, indeed, be retrogressive in view of the considerable scientific progress effected contemporaneously with the passing of the initial internationalism. Nevertheless, taking into account the existence of higher education, which is for the most part nationalistic, it is, without a doubt, necessary to develop its international dimensions.

The international opening of higher education consists, in the first place, of an appreciation of the wealth of human consciousness. Cultural systems have the habit of becoming circumscribed within the restricted parameters plotted by a civilization which is historically and linguistically defined, corresponding to an area of language, a political system, or even a state. This temptation of the exclusion of others is a serious problem, on occasion fatal. It can be explained by the sentiment of superiority held with regard to that which is different. Totalitarian regimes, as evidenced particularly by the Marxist countries, try to avoid contacts which might show up their shortcomings and disturb the exclusive domination they seek to exercise over their subjects. It should also be noted that, in certain cases, the rejection of foreign exchanges is a reaction of weakness on the part of those who feel unable to bear comparison. For those who believe in the extraordinary wealth of human consciousness, who are convinced that every culture has an irreplaceable value, that the experience of others is always interesting, and that progress is born of the exchange, it is essential to work towards the ever-widening of the various fields of knowledge.

International higher education supposes, in the second place, the development of comparative studies. This is particularly so in those sectors of research which carry a national mark of cultural originality: literature, the arts, philosophy, law, economics, and political science. Please excuse this professor of constitutional law for expressing his particular regret at the general shortage of comparative studies in law and government; increased efforts are called for here.

In the third place, cultural exchanges of students and teachers should be encouraged. Only in this way can higher education be seen to be international. Initiatives in this field are, to date, insufficient, notwithstanding the success of certain programs such as the Education Abroad Program of the University of California.

University exchanges come up against numerous obstacles. Economic restrictions weigh heavily. People of the rich nations, or the wealthier members of virtually any country, have the means to study abroad, but it is generally impossible for others. And, this inequality reinforces initial differences. It is also necessary to take account of the administrative difficulties which prevent a student from working abroad and from benefitting from this work in his national university career. Certain education systems are more accessible than others, as is the case in the United States, and efforts are underway, notably within the European Community, to remove the numerous obstacles which remain and are related to the existence of cultural, political and, particularly, linguistic barriers.

How can these difficulties be overcome? It would be somewhat naive to imagine that complete remedies can be found for this chronic and serious affliction. Several options may, nevertheless, be canvassed. Among the industrialized nations, the improvement of the international character of higher education is a product of the setting up of a tightly knit network of exchange conventions between universities, allowing for greater mobility of both teachers and students. Inter-university exchange conventions offer a threefold advantage: that of giving to each party the responsibility of choosing that sector in which the two institutions have interests in common; that of guaranteeing for both students and teachers a reception worked out by both parties; and that of giving to the exchange a human importance which will serve to strengthen the personalities involved. Conventions of this kind exist, but there should be more of them. Technical problems may arise, but are not beyond resolution.

The universities of the industrialized world have a service to render to those of non-industrialized countries. It is not simply a question of aid but also one of exchange which must, and can, be balanced as all the parties have something to offer. The methods of this exchange are difficult to establish, as they need to encompass both individual needs and those of the nation as a whole. An international higher education which serves simply to remove the elite of a particular developing country, or as a means to disseminate an alien culture, would be a failure. It has been known to occur in the past, and we should guard against any repetition.

The conviction held by the majority of universities of the international character of higher education is, of course, vital, but, in itself, insufficient. To institute this principle will demand considerable efforts. Our job here is to put forward and discuss new and effective solutions.

4
Higher Education Is International

Barbara B. Burn

I am pleased that my topic is so affirmative, rather than, for example, "Higher Education Should Be International," or worse, "Is Higher Education International?" I am also pleased that the topic has a universal character, that it is not "American Higher Education Is International." That would be too parochial.

In discussing our topic, I shall focus mainly on why higher education is international and to a lesser extent on how one measures this and, assuming there are degrees of internationality in higher education, how it can be maximized. It should be noted that I refer not to the internationalization of higher education, but to its internationality, a word which, according to Webster's Second Edition, means "the quality or state of being international." This is deliberate as the word internationalization implies moving from non-international to internationality. My topic and my convictions rule out the possibility that higher education is non-international, though it may have varying degrees of internationality.

Why Is Higher Education International?

The origin of the Ph.D. degree in Great Britain suggests one factor that impels higher education to be international. When Lord Balfour, British Foreign Secretary, made a goodwill mission to the United States during the First World War, he discovered that much of the American leadership had gained familiarity with Germany as a consequence of pursuing advanced study in that country. On returning to Britain, he persuaded the University of London to offer the Ph.D., until then resisted in Britain as a "Germanic novelty," so that future American leadership would be drawn to Britain for postgraduate study.

International educational exchange builds important ties between nations. The internationality of higher education is for this reason a matter of deliberate public policy on the part of many countries. In this connection it is worth noting that according to the U.S. Department of State about 63,000 Third World students are currently pursuing studies in the Soviet Union and Eastern Europe, supported by these countries and governments at a cost of around $325 million annually. In 1980-1981 the federal government of the United States supported only 6,000-7,000 foreign nationals for study at American colleges and universities, including the Fulbright and Agency for International Development programs. If, as our former Ambassador to Italy, Richard N. Gardner, recently stated, "'Public diplomacy' has to do with assuring an effectively functioning 'intellectual connection' between one's own and foreign countries"[1], the United States lags in this field compared to many other countries. But whether funded by public or private monies, higher education is international because it is a vehicle for fostering intellectual connections.

A second reason why higher education is international can be summarized by the phrase "international intellectual borrowing." The essence of this phenomenon was vividly conveyed by the comment of the chairman of a major American high tech firm (who shall remain anonymous) when he ascribed Japan's competitive advantage over the U.S. in some high tech fields to the fact that "the Japanese have people running all over the labs at MIT, Stanford, and Caltech." It is not accidental that a high proportion of American faculty who were awarded Senior Von Humboldt Fellowships by West Germany are in science and engineering. This is a deliberate and enlightened strategy of reverse brain drain.

I had the opportunity to witness "international borrowing" at the undergraduate level when I recently evaluated the University of California's Education Abroad Program in Padua in connection with the reaccreditation review of UC Santa Barbara. I was intrigued to learn that one UC student was studying orchestral conducting at the G.B. Martini Music Conservatory in Bologna, a short commute from Padua. I would cite this as a fine example of international borrowing.

There are other examples of international borrowing among nations which make higher education international. May I cite two. The first is that about one-fourth of new faculty hired in American engineering schools are foreign-born. Secondly, an objective of the Commonwealth Higher Education Programme of the Association of Commonwealth Universities is to encourage the development of Centres for Advanced Study and Research within the developing Commonwealth countries, the purpose being to attract the best students and scholars to these regional resources and to serve them efficiently. International borrowing gives a hunting license to colleges and universities to recruit faculty and students worldwide irrespective of national origins, thus underscoring the internationality of higher education.

These Commonwealth centers reflect yet another rationale for the internationality of higher education, namely, to enhance quality in higher education. Just as it is neither feasible nor cost-effective for educational resources to be spread evenly within the higher education systems of individual countries, so at the international level, for reasons of cost and quality, a rationalization of centers of excellence worldwide makes higher education institutions international, especially the best universities and the best departments and institutes within them.

The People's Republic of China gives explicit recognition to this reality by providing special support to its seventy-plus "key" universities and research institutes to enable them to bring in foreign scholars from abroad and to support their own scholars for advanced study and research in other countries. Scholarly productivity requires a critical mass of outstanding colleagues and it is eminently reasonable that the best scholars concentrate at the leading centers for teaching and research worldwide or make periodic safaris to them, for example, to the campuses of the University of California.

The correlation between internationality and quality was affirmed by the study done of the American professoriate a few years ago by Ladd and Lipset.[2] They found that whereas 57 percent of all American academics had never ventured professionally outside the United States, 71 percent of the faculty members at major research universities in this country had been abroad professionally. Research which I recently completed on the contribution that their sojourn in the Federal Republic of Germany made to American Fulbrighters professionally as well as personally, further affirms the relationship between quality and internationality in higher education. Former American Fulbrighters to West Germany (and to other Western European countries also surveyed in my study) have a much more substantial record of scholarly research and publication than the average American academic. Scholarly productivity and international mobility go together in higher education, thus internationalizing the leading institutions worldwide.

In addition to the three factors so far mentioned which make higher education international -- building intellectual connections among nations, intellectual borrowing, and the quality of higher education -- a fourth factor is increasingly important. This is the interdependence of countries and the internationalization of most professions. To function effectively today the professional in a growing range of fields requires a knowledge of other countries and their languages, of international issues, and of the developments abroad which shape the day-to-day exigencies that he or she faces in dealing with the in-box inflow.

Flora Lewis, a well-known newspaper correspondent, referred to this growing interdependence recently when she noted the need for recognition that:

> Economic factors are all linked and cannot be resolved in isolation. Sagging trade, international debt, currency movements, credits, interest rates, the unregulated slosh of the nearly trillion-dollar Eurodollar pool, feed each other and aggravate the world recession.
>
> Domestic U.S. economic decisions have not only a direct effect on everybody else, the third world as well as America's industrial partners, but also that others affect U.S. prospects.[3]

Thus higher education must be more and more international so that it prepares professionals to function in an international context, especially, but not only, in the fields of business, trade, and finance. Among other pertinent fields are public health, agriculture, social services, and the law. Unfortunately, the United States lags in this effort compared to some other countries. In Japan, for example, the Ministry of Education supports international educational exchanges which send young Japanese undergraduates to American colleges and universities for a year, not just to take courses and learn American approaches to various disciplines, notably economics and political science, but also to enable these students to become acquainted with American culture and with American students who in the future may well be their professional counterparts and colleagues. In this, as in other fields, the Japanese demonstrate an enlightened and long-range view.

The European Economic Community (EEC) has also shown an appreciation of the internationalization of many professions through its support of what is called the Joint Programs of Study. In existence since the late 1970s, this scheme encourages the exchange of students and faculty and the development of joint degree programs among institutions of higher education in the EEC through providing start-up funding. The students' study abroad is an integral part of their degree -- in some cases they earn degrees from both their home and host institutions -- rather than an "add-on" to their basic academic program for purposes of pursuing culture and language study, as still tends to be all too common in American study abroad programs. The notion is that many professional fields, for example, engineering and business studies, are international, and the academic programs preparing for them must similarly be international.

International interdependence has another facet which also reinforces the internationality of higher education: the international interdependence of research. Kenneth Prewitt, president of the Social Science Research Council (SSRC), focused on this in his preface to SSRC's Annual Report of 1981-1982 in reference to foreign area studies, but his comments apply to an increasing range of academic fields. His statement that "area scholarship has become something which colleagues across national borders do together"[4] applies well beyond area studies. To be specific, what he said about the committee structure of the American Council for Learned Societies (ACLS) and the SSRC, which encourages area studies research, applies equally to the role of higher education institutions in fostering the internationalization of many fields of scholarship and hence of higher education worldwide.

With respect to these committees Prewitt stated that they "have become import-export structures, seeking out and incorporating into American scholarship the best research going on elsewhere, as well as sharing American-conducted research with colleagues."[5] This international interdependence of research is thus another factor in making higher education international. It is, of course, closely related to the factors already mentioned: intellectual connections, intellectual borrowing, and scholarly quality.

Indices of Internationality

My remarks so far have been mostly positive in affirming our topic, "Higher Education Is International." How do we measure its internationality? On this I want to emphasize only one main point: the degree to which institutions of higher education are international cannot be measured on the basis of international mobility. For example, criteria often used are numbers of foreign students enrolled (and there are currently more than 326,000 in the United States), numbers of faculty exchanges with other countries, or numbers of college courses in international relations and area studies and foreign languages and the enrollments in them. However, statistics on these matters show little. Crucial to whether or not higher education is international is how we exploit the international mobility of students and scholars and the knowledge and motivation students gain from their international courses.

In these respects much more effort is needed. The presence of foreign students and scholars in our midst may even make for a greater anti-foreign sentiment than if they stayed home. We need to orchestrate their presence to turn American students "on" rather than "off" about the rest of the world. As president of the National Association for Foreign Student Affairs (NAFSA), I am deeply concerned that international exchanges of students and college and university policies towards foreign students have such an apparently low priority in central decision-making in too many higher education institutions. Too often these visitors are regarded as an aggravation rather than as a resource for international learning and reinforcing the internationality of our institutions. NAFSA is making a major effort to encourage colleges and universities to develop institutional policies on international educational exchange, but more effort is needed.

How to Maximize Internationality in Higher Education?

Much has happened in higher education worldwide in the last decade to intensify its internationality. International student flows have tripled worldwide. The flow of faculty between countries has not increased commensurately but has grown, although we lack statistics to document this. In the U.S. we are now more concerned than a few years ago about the need to strengthen foreign language and international studies, a need documented by the President's Commission on Foreign Language and International Studies in its report to President Carter in November 1979. Awareness of the need has reached a new level in our national consciousness, which is not to say that the need is anywhere near being met, or that it is a priority with the Reagan administration.

In my view, a major lack in the work of the President's Commission was the fact that it was a national rather than an international effort. It is by definition not possible to strengthen the internationality of higher education in one country unless this is a collaborative undertaking with other countries around the globe. Strengthening the internationality of higher education must be reciprocal and multinational.

NOTES

1. Richard N. Gardner, "Selling America in the Marketplace of Ideas," New York Times Sunday Magazine, 20 March 1983, p.2.

2. Everett C. Ladd, Jr. and Seymour Martin Lipset, "Faculty Members Who Travel Abroad," Chronicle of Higher Education, 24 April 1978, p.8.

3. Flora Lewis, "Seize the Moment," The New York Times, 14 December 1983, p.A 31.

4. Annual Report of Social Science Research Council (SSRC) of 1981-1982 (New York: SSRC), p.xxii.

5. Ibid.

5
Aspects of the Internationalization of Higher Education

A: THE UNIVERSITY IN THE THIRD WORLD

An African Perspective
Ampah Johnson

Inter-university cooperation is a uniting factor that brings together different people and even different civilizations. It can be initiated by university officials, political leaders, or by individuals, such as professors working in institutions of higher education. It is, perhaps, the only area in which cooperation is carried out between equal partners and without a spirit of domination or hegemony. It is, moreover, of reciprocal benefit. It is explained, perhaps, by the specific nature of the university, where teaching and research are founded on the strict respect of truth and where genuine practice of tolerance and mutual respect is the order of the day.

In connection with the value of inter-university cooperation, Dr. William H. Allaway, Director of the University of California Education Abroad Program pointed out at the 1980 meeting of the International Association of Universities in Manila that the contributions of the Third World universities to the universities of the rich countries should not go unrecognized and that it would be wrong to underestimate the intellectual and cultural advantages that accrue from time spent within another culture and, in certain areas, the productivity of research carried out in a different environment. Dr. Allaway went on to report that the University of California has signed exchange agreements with several African universities that enable it to send students to study in Africa for a year, and under which African graduate students can study on one of the UC campuses.

Several years ago the University of Benin and the University of California signed an agreement of cooperation. The understanding was that the University of Benin would admit students from California who were participants in the Education Abroad Program while students from the University of Benin would come to study in the California system. In accordance with the initial agreement, about a dozen UC students spent the second semester of the academic year at the University of Benin, following a semester of language and African studies at the University of Bordeaux.

Research programs carefully thought out and carried through by researchers from the two universities are another aspect of our cooperation. In this respect, also, the cooperation between our two universities has borne fruit. Archaeological excavations carried out in Togo in 1979 and in 1980 by a team of researchers from UCLA and the University of Benin, led by Professor Merrick Posnansky, yielded a rich harvest. Some objects discovered are the vestiges of living places that are believed to be some of the oldest in West Africa. What is even more important is that artifacts were discovered in the region of Notse that were similar to others discovered much earlier in the area of Benin City in Nigeria, thus confirming the theory relating to the migration of people from the Niger Delta to southern Togo.

What education means in the life of a country was brought into evidence by Thomas Jefferson, who was President of the United States from 1801 to 1809. May I paraphrase from some of his statements:

> I am much prouder to have been the founder of the University of Virginia than to have been the President of the United States. The possession of an enlightened and developed mind is the best guarantee we can have for running a political system founded on the free consent of those who are governed. If this idea fails, then all the dollars of the world yielded by taxes will not suffice to prevent a nation from turning against itself.

The University of California is celebrating its 115th anniversary, and the Education Abroad Program, its 20th anniversary. I should offer it my congratulations on its outstanding achievements. One hundred and fifteen years is a long time in the existence of a university; however, this is a relatively short time when compared with the overall span of the educational enterprise. I say this because the present-day institutions of higher education, as they engage in the search for and transmission of knowledge, are following a tradition that is deeply rooted in the distant past. Though the connection may be somewhat loose, the Palace, or Palatine School that flourished under Charlemagne in France during the eighth century might be considered as a remote ancestor of the university, indicating that as far back as the eighth century schools existed whose aim was the extension and improvement of education. But, it was really in the twelfth century that what is now the modern university came to be established. According to the Jesuit priest, Frederic Copleston, the greatest of all the medieval universities was unquestionably that of Paris. Soon thereafter other universities, such as Oxford and Bologna, came into prominence and began to display a spirit of their own. The developing and expanding intellectual life of the period showed itself in the first attempts at the classification and systematization of knowledge. The charter, granted either by pope or emperor, that established a university, conferred considerable privileges on professors and students. The two most important privileges were those of internal jurisdiction and of the power to give a degree, which carried with it the license to teach.

Today, in the twentieth century, we jealously guard these privileges in the name of academic freedom. The university in the twelfth century was a largely independent and closed corporation which maintained its privileges against church and state. Today, universities have, to a greater or lesser extent, maintained that character of independence. This explains why, in spite of deliberate attempts at relevance, present-day universities are sometimes referred to, or even castigated, as ivory tower institutions. Let them be so.

In Africa south of the Sahara, the part of the Third World with which I am best acquainted, the first attempts at university education led to the creation of Fourah Bay College in Sierra Leone, West Africa, and of Makerere College in Uganda, East Africa. For several years, these two universities remained the first generation of universities. From the late 1940s, in keeping with the great awakening that found expression in the accession to full sovereignty and independence by formerly dependent people, the second-generation universities came into being. As in many other parts of the Third World, African universities have come to stay.

The mission of the university in the Third World must be to educate, that is, to disseminate knowledge, for knowledge is the decisive resource for overall human development and democratic life. A wide distribution of knowledge can raise literacy levels and improve food production, health and sanitation standards, and address other human needs. The university in the Third World must also endeavor, where adequate financial resources are available, to discover new knowledge through research and, finally, to render services to the community in which it is implanted. It must stress excellence.

We agree, therefore, that the mission of the university in the Third World cannot be different from that of universities in the industrialized countries. But, in carrying out its mission, the university in the Third World should seek to be relevant; that is, the development that it seeks to bring about through education must be compatible with the culture of the land and with the deepest aspirations of the people.

The former President of Senegal, Leopold Senghor, once noted that cultural independence, in the sense of the will to think and act by oneself for oneself, is the condition sine qua non for any other form of independence, the political one included. He felt that if effective solutions are to be found to political and economic problems, then both politicians and economists should affirm with greater insistence that they pay more attention to their culture.

Let me say something about culture. Culture is the way of life of a human group. It includes all the learned and standardized forms of behavior which are recognized and used within the group. The elegance, refinement and advancement in the style of living that have come to characterize the culture of Western society are developments due, in large measure, to the application of technology. To my mind, this explains why the people of the Third World are also stressing technology as the one important factor of development. That is the way it should be. But, the temptation so far has been to import technology that is already available in the industrialized world, and now the talk is about the transfer of technology. Certainly, science and technology can be brought to bear in the setting of the Third World to help meet the basic needs of the people. However, I do not think that the solution lies fully in the transfer into the Third World of technology developed in the industrialized countries.

The question may be asked as to what current technology from the industrialized countries will be useful in the Third World over a long period of time. The technologies of the industrialized countries are, of course, designed to suit environments or conditions that are different from those prevailing in much of the Third World. Therefore, I am of the opinion that the technologies that the Third World needs are appropriate technologies provided that they are based on local energy and human resources. Those countries in the Third World which are able to train their own scientists and engineers and develop their own energy sources will progress rapidly. The university in the Third World has an extremely important role to play in this endeavor. It must bring all of its intellectual resources to bear on the training, under local conditions, of the manpower necessary for development. Through research, the university must lead the way in helping to develop local, renewable energy sources. With the bold leadership of its universities, the Third World should be self-reliant and should avoid the mere imitation of historic developments in the industrialized world.

When I call on the Third World to be self-reliant, I do not mean to suggest that it should stand in isolation from the rest of the world. Such an attitude would be suicidal, for, as is evidenced by the global reach of the present economic crisis, what characterizes the modern world is the interdependence of nations. While he was speaking at the inaugural session of The World Economic Conference held in London in June, 1933, the late King George V said, and I quote:

> It cannot be beyond the power of man so to use the vast resources of the world as to ensure the material progress of civilization. No diminution in these resources has taken place; on the contrary, discovery, invention and localization have multiplied their possibilities to such an extent that abundance of production has itself created new problems. And, together with this amazing material progress, there has come a new recognition of the interdependence of nations and of the value of collaboration between them. Now is the opportunity to harness this new consciousness of common interest to the service of mankind.[1]

Bretton Woods may, in a sense, be considered as an answer to that call to harness the consciousness of common interests to the service of mankind. The world had gone through an economic depression. At Bretton Woods, an attempt was made to give collective attention and management to the world economy. Since I am not an economist, I shall not venture a judgment on whether or not the hopes of those who met at Bretton Woods were realized. But, it is indeed true to say that, at the time, the world was divided into two main groups: the industrialized North, and a South that was in a state of economic and political dependence. The interests of the South were ignored. That South has now emerged from political dependence and is trying to build its economy. The call, as we approach the end of the twentieth century, is for a new international economic order that continues to give collective attention to the world economy and that is founded on concern for both the poor and the rich.

A North-South dialogue has been instituted, an example of which is the series of negotiations that culminated in the signing of the now famous Yaounde and Lome Conventions between the European Economic Community and the African-Caribbean-Pacific countries. Given its enormous intellectual capacity, the Third World university has a specific role to play in shedding light on the issues involved in the dialogue between the North and the South.

I have come to the point where I shall attempt to summarize what I have said so far. The university in the Third World must be at the forefront of, indeed, must enlighten and must lead, the planned transformation that is called development. That is why the tendency in all the Third World universities is for them to be like melting pots open to all streams of thought -- with a view to the kind of cooperation as will result in maximum mutual benefit. They, the universities in the Third World, are disposed to draw the best from all cultural systems in order to create a synthesis that will play a significant part in strengthening their own personalities and be the basis of their own contributions, however modest, to the universal cultural heritage.

NOTES

1. Ramphall Sridath, "No Time to Lose," Development Forum, December 1982 (United Nations University and the Division of Economic and Social Information), p.16.

A Western Perspective

John A. Marcum

Today we are seriously threatened by the danger of closing boundaries and closing minds. If this danger mounts within the Western community, how much greater it is between the West and the Third World! How much more precarious the linkages, how much more difficult to sustain and to maintain mobility across the boundaries between the West and the Third World. The loss of contact, the handicap of mutual incomprehension, the danger of protectionism of the mind as well as of economics, are real.

I find it especially challenging to confront these dangers within the context of where we are meeting. I can imagine that it may be particularly difficult for the gentle joggers of Santa Barbara to make the vicarious leap necessary to engage the problems of the external world. This is such a beautiful, soft, warm, healthy, supremely Californian and Western context. The Third World could scarcely be farther away. Even the realities and problems of our own society seem distant. Thus, there is the need for an extraordinary effort to cross the comprehension gap. And therefore, the importance of facing the fact that contact with external reality may become increasingly more difficult.

I am convinced of the importance of exposure to the Third World. My own initial exposure was through an organization, the Experiment in International Living, back in 1957. As a young instructor (almost still a student), I went to Black Africa for the first time -- initially to the University of Ibadan. Our Experiment group learned much from its exposure to that Third World university. In fact, at that time the University of Ibadan was still a colonial institution where English literature was taught but *economics was not*. This said something important about the colonial period, the realities of Nigerian society, and what might happen in the future.

Two years later in 1959, it was my privilege to attend the first lectures on African history given by an African historian at the University of Dakar, Senegal. Joseph Kizerbo gave his pioneering, Afro-centric version of what had always been presented before as colonial history or African history as viewed from France. It was an exhilarating experience for an outsider. It must have been even more so for African students. It was also a dramatic illustration of how, as an outsider at a Third World university, one can learn much about what is happening and changing in another intellectual world, and gain an important insight into that world's social dynamics.

Third World universities are complex hybrids of history: they are partly colonial and they are partly creatures of indigenous national and local cultural traditions. Where divisive ethnic pressures are strong, they are subject to tendencies or pressures to become parochial, that is, to become sub-national. They are fulcrums of intellectual questioning and often difficult, strenuous and strained environments where political protest may develop and pose difficult problems for outsiders.

The University of California, in pursuing the theme of education as international, should value the importance of relationships with Third World universities. But, it needs to do so in a realistic way. Students who go to Third World universities must be well-prepared, well-oriented, steeled for uncertainties and inflexibilities of curriculum. They will not find the open smorgasbord or easy-to-talk-your-way-in-and-out-of requirements which are characteristic of many an American institution. There will be things they will not like or to which they can not easily adjust but that need not be a block to learning. One can learn how to cope with the problem of scarce resources. Library facilities and laboratories will not be what they are here. But, in the process of coping -- and I saw it with the UC students in Ghana in 1974, when the university closed down the very night that I arrived to look at the Education Abroad Program there -- one *can* find that aside from all of the things that one learns in a formal way, Third World experience helps to develop a self-reliance and resourcefulness that one would *never* have the occasion to develop in the beautiful context of *Santa* Barbara, or for that matter, Santa Cruz, Los Angeles, or other UC campuses.

Such rigors, of course, confront EAP faculty directors at the various UC study centers with great responsibility. I will never cease to marvel at the performance of Professor Donald Rothchild of UC Davis, who handled the university closure in Ghana with aplomb and resourcefulness. All of his students learned something extremely valuable, namely the importance of posing and facing daunting and difficult questions. As a student or as a visiting professor in alien, Third World circumstances, one must learn how to be resilient and sympathetic, learn how to understand without being intrusive. One must recognize that one is not *of* a host country, but is of a larger international or world community. One must sort out what, under the circumstances, is an appropriate or inappropriate response. One must learn to cope with the sort of demanding eventualities for which preparation for studying in the Third World can alert us.

I believe we are talking about a scarce resource, something that might even be disappearing. If one looks at the enrollments in the Education Abroad Program in the Third World universities, they are slight. Opportunities for establishing and maintaining those relationships may become fewer. Unless we make seizing these opportunities a high priority, we may lose a very precious resource. The situation calls for a constancy of relationships and it certainly calls for reciprocity in these relationships. Reciprocity may appropriately vary in different circumstances. But it certainly means that we have a responsibility to help those universities develop their own resources and their own faculties by means of expanding research access and cooperation in both directions; that is, in opening our institutions to researchers from those countries and, we hope, receiving in return and, as appropriate, reciprocating research opportunities. Again, these relationships may become very difficult to preserve unless we are proactive.

In summary, there is an intensity of experience open to Westerners in Third World universities, a particular "shock of recognition," especially for people who are growing up in a world of television and fast foods. We are discussing a dimension of the world that we dare not lose contact with and that we must, for our own society's and the world's sake, learn how to cope with in a creative way lest that gap of mutual incomprehension grow beyond remedy.

Thus, it would be my own hope that this university and other American and Western institutions pay particular attention, at a time when all the pressures are in the opposite direction, to sustaining and nourishing interchange, not just among themselves and the Western world but across that other boundary -- to Asia, to Latin America, to Africa. We need to search together and to find new modes of constructive interaction.

B: THE UNDERGRADUATE DIMENSION

Differences in Academic Traditions
Ralf Dahrendorf

Since I am the head of an institution in which almost 50 percent of the students are graduates, I am rather surprised to be a discussant in a group on undergraduate education. Worse than that, whenever a student asks me whether he should go abroad and, if so, when, I invariably say that there are advantages in going abroad after the first degree. It makes much sense to go abroad as a postgraduate once one has a firm base in the university system from which one comes. I had better make this confession before entering into a discussion of undergraduate education and its international aspects.

Professor Lavroff has reminded us (Ed. note: Chapter 3) that at the outset universities, being seats of scholarship, were naturally international. Insofar as we are involved in scholarship, internationalism is built into what we are doing. One hardly needs to talk about it. It is not a question of exchanging people, or at least, not primarily a question of exchanging people; it is a question of doing our job of trying to find out the causes of things. This is something that we cannot do by limiting ourselves to whatever is being published within the confines of a particular national culture.

Professor Lavroff went on to say that the nation-state, and the emergence of the nation-state, changed this fundamental internationalism of scholarship. The universities became part of a new concept of the nation-state and there is a national flavor, or cultural flavor, to universities wherever we go. I think he made some very important remarks about a subject which is part of our concern, that is, the position of universities in the new nation-states, and the problems which arise for them: how they become instruments of power, or at any rate, instruments of constraint.

Moving on to our own time leads me to a controversial question which I believe we should discuss: Does what we believe about the intrinsic internationalism of scholarship, and does what we believe about the essence of universities in the old sense, really apply in the same way after the tremendous period of expansion which we have gone through in Europe in the last decades and in the United States much earlier? Does the old type of internationalism of academic education really apply to the tens or hundreds of thousands of students as it did to the hundreds or the thousands? I think this is a very important, but not a very easy question to answer.

Now, let me mention a word about undergraduate education and international exchange. One of the characteristics of the world university system is that there are two different traditions, and two totally different ways of dealing with undergraduates. There is, on the one hand, the British and American tradition, which in a sense is based on the ossified university of the late Middle Ages. This type of university was actually quite bad and second-rate in the nineteenth century, and not very alive; but it is a university which, by structuring undergraduate education, has actually been better able to absorb growing numbers of students than the other type of university which is found on the European continent. On the European continent, there is a totally different tradition by which the unity of research and teaching is maintained, at least as a fiction, a tradition which made our continental universities immensely lively places of creative scholarship in the nineteenth century. It is a tradition, however, which today in a world in which higher education has expanded, does not provide undergraduates with the same kind of structured opportunity of learning which exists in the Anglo-American tradition. This is a very important difference and, incidentally, an important technical difference if one is concerned with exchanging students. That is to say, it is never easy to tell at what stage an undergraduate from one system should go to the other system. It is characteristic of the Continental system that, on the one hand, you do not quite know when you are going to finish your studies and get your degree; and, on the other hand, you feel that if you leave your country you lose out on your vocational opportunities.

It is characteristic of the British and American systems -- more the British than the American system, to the advantage of the American one -- that within the three years which it takes to get the first degree there is hardly the time or the opportunity to go abroad.

In my experience, the result is, and I return to my initial question about the desirability of exchanging undergraduates, that it is quite easy, welcome, and highly effective to exchange undergraduates from American universities with four-year undergraduate programs. It is also my experience that those who come to Europe for a year have generally benefitted. In terms of the London School of Economics, I can certainly state that the institution benefits from the fact that about 180 American students come for one year from universities with four-year undergraduate courses. They are lively, interesting, and on the average somewhat above the already high level of students we have.

We also have a similar number of students who come from the Continental system. They enjoy getting tutorials and being in a totally different type of educational system and probably benefit in less tangible ways.

Thus, I remain with the double question: a) Does the belief in exchange at the undergraduate level apply to the vastly expanded educational systems of today as it did in earlier centuries? and b) Is there not, perhaps, a case for concentrating exchanges on postgraduates rather than undergraduates in international exchanges?

Understanding the Complexities of Another Culture

Dennis C. McElrath

The heart of the character and quality of the undergraduate experience abroad is that some small part of the world has been made real, whole, complex, changing, and personal. I do not know how this can be accomplished in a normal classroom or even a tutorial. It is, indeed, a part of the overseas experience.

Perhaps the most important parts of the experience are the students' sense of the complexities of the other culture and their understanding of the complexities. By this, I mean that they come away with a sense, not simply that other peoples are similar to or different from them or that other value systems are similar or different, but of the hierarchies of values -- the priorities of values that operate in the society that they are visiting. Thus, as I reflect on my own experience as a study center director in Italy and think about what values I and the students at the center came away with, I can say that no one can sustain an experience in an Italian university over a period of time without leaving with a sense of several important, major values and the priorities in Italian society. For example, it seems to me that the centrality of the family in Italian life is something which enters every facet of every discussion. The importance of place and locality is another. Also, there is the profound, deep, abiding mistrust of central government and its agencies; the tyranny of the bureaucracy. It appears to me the other side of that is the ubiquitousness of politics. Politics enters into every facet of intellectual life, every conversation, every analysis of every situation, every piece of art, and every film. All issues are cast politically. Just as I suppose the natural bent of the English would be to cast something into a class analysis, so the Italians will cast almost every discussion into a political one.

In looking back, then, on that experience and the way in which my students experienced it, it seems to me that we might want to think about how to enhance the ability of the overseas experience to provide the student with the kind of insight into a different culture, as will enable him or her to gain an understanding of priorities, and the hierarchies of values and norms in that culture. Among the thoughts that occur to me in this regard is that values tend to be expressed in hierarchical form when a choice is forced on someone; that is, when you see them in operation and are required to choose one way or the other. That kind of choosing occurs in a living situation. It happens over and over again as you talk to other students in the host country and as you try to defend your own ideas, and so on.

I think that the sense of the hierarchy of values requires an exposure to a great variety of situations in a foreign culture. We are all, I am sure, trying to figure out whether Margaret Mead was right. Did she look just at one little corner of one little society in Samoa, or should she have wandered around and experienced the coming of age in a great variety of situations so that she could sort out those characteristics which are universal and part of a culture, and those which are particular and situational? It seems to me that a sustained overseas experience for a student allows for that kind of understanding. It allows you to somehow sort out those universals and those particulars within a culture, if you stay for a while and you become involved.

Also, as I look back on my experiences and those of my students, I realize that an understanding of the hierarchy of values, and of the priorities that are set within a society, comes from passionate debate. Students are passionate human beings, and part of the overseas experience is to engage them in this intellectual discourse. That passion of debate and the heat of it forces people to confront different values and the complexity of those values.

Finally, at some point in the overseas experience of students, there should be moments for reflection on what it is all about, and what is happening to them and in their lives. At some point, they have to withdraw from the passion.

Anyway, these thoughts do not answer the question as to whether or not the overseas experience can handle large scale societies or societies of increasing scale and larger numbers of students. But, they do address other issues.

C: COLLABORATIVE RESEARCH AND FACULTY EXCHANGE

A View from Italy

Louise George Clubb

I will concentrate on the possibilities for collaborative research at Italian universities, not only because I have recently returned from directing the University of California Education Abroad Program in Padua but because that experience underscored, as nothing else could, both the opportunities and the importance of international academic exchange.

Humanists, on the whole, tend to be loners more than do scientists. Although we are no less in touch with people, many of these people are dead, and therefore we can encounter them by ourselves in libraries. In all the years I've been going to Italy -- first as a junior year abroad student not quite sure of what I was studying, and later on with research grants, very sure what I was studying and exactly how many weeks I was going to put in at this library or that, speaking only to librarians or to colleagues who also were doing individual research in Italy -- I never fully envisaged the possibilities of collaborative research until I became UC Director at the University of Padua, with links to the University of Venice, to the Accademia of Venice and to the Martini Conservatory of Bologna. And I have constantly observed in conversations with the faculty members who teach the UC students and with those who recommend the Italian students who come to the UC campuses on the reciprocity program, that what our host universities and other host institutions, in Italy at any rate, are most interested in is raising the level -- not the level of quality, but the level of category or stage of advancement -- of the exchange programs.

In Italy the undergraduate student is viewed benignly but is not, to the Italian mind, fully a member of the academic community. The graduate student (or the Italian equivalent, the thesis-writer) is where the real action is, student-wise. Faculty members cultivate coteries of advanced students; they dream of sending them for a time to an appropriate campus of the University of California, where often they also dream of going themselves. I had not fully realized until living in Padua that these desires had been relatively unfulfilled by the aims of the EAP simply because the EAP had not realized that, in the case of Italy, they are not talking about the same level of exchange. The Italian universities have recently established a degree corresponding to the Ph.D., the Dottorato di Ricerca. It is beginning now to function in selected university istituti or departments. This is one of the ways in which international education internationalizes. This particular effect occured early in England. In Italy, one of the reasons for putting in this new degree program was doubtless a desire to function on an equal footing in the hierarchy of degree programs with the United States and other countries that have the Ph.D., so that Italian graduate students might earn credit for courses taken abroad.

One of the two major points to be made about collaborative research with the University of Padua and other Italian institutions is that it is already in progress. Professor Dahrendorf (Ed. note: Chapter 2) mentioned his conviction that small is beautiful but large is necessary. With collaborative research and faculty exchange, I think, the delicate balance between small and large, the ideal that Castiglione called a difficult mediocrita, a golden mean, must be achieved by attention to alternation as the occasion demands. Collaborative research programs must be small, in that they must respond to a precise and specific need, not merely grow from the generally agreed-upon principle that it is a very good thing to exchange ideas, that international travel and study enlarge the mind and make for broader productivity and political understanding, and so on. A serious program begins, rather, with an individual scholar and his graduate students, as well as undergraduate students, who will gather around graduate students just as graduate students will gather around a professor when there is a particular subject to be studied, a particular course offered at the university or a particular thesis or project to which the assignments of the individual members of the equipe can contribute. The inter-relation of the levels of exchange programs, and the superiority of the personal exchange to the exchange which begins with a certain number of slots, on the one hand, to be matched by a certain number of tickets, on the other, is the larger side of the alternation between small and large that I am recommending. There is a network of relationships that goes from undergraduate students to graduate students to faculty, visiting professors and researchers. International education programs really do not function best when they are compartmentalized, as they are so often. The junior year abroad student does take a course or two, but is mainly occupied in meeting other junior year abroad students or foreign students at the same level, and is frequently cut off from the higher levels of the academic life of the host university. At the University of Padua, California students often feel diffident about going to hear a lecturer, even a visiting UC professor, if the lecture is being offered outside their own immediate undergraduate sphere and if they have no acquaintance with more advanced students and assistenti who are at the center of the academic action in the seminars of the various departments.

On the one hand, I see the exchange programs that UC might encourage as being aimed at emphasizing the diversity of the levels and ways in which studies can be connected so that students abroad are not isolated from other age groups or other levels of research; but, on the other hand, emphasizing the smallness, never losing sight of the individual and of the very specific goal. I'll take two kinds of exchanges, one long realized and the other recently undertaken, as examples of possible collaborative research. The first, at the University of Padua, is research in peptides, begun on a personal basis between the Paduan Professor of Chemistry, Ernesto Scoppone and UC San Diego Professor Murray Goodman. For many years, as researchers interested in the same thing, having met through their discipline, they built a connection that has resulted in something that has outlived Professor Scoppone, but has, under Professor Goodman's aegis, become a regular exchange between San Diego and Padua, concentrated not on scientific research, in general, but specifically on peptides research. Graduate students, and junior and senior faculty are constantly engaged in coming and going to discuss peptides, without dependence on any one system or particular exchange program. Although Italians used to be notorious for not learning foreign languages well, today's Paduan peptides' chemists speak English fluently, but with a southern California accent, if there is such a thing. That is one kind of collaborative research, small in organization and long-enduring; growing, also, because the field of peptides is expanding.

The second kind of specific program is almost accidental. When I went to Padua several years ago, I had just launched a series at UC involving textual research and new translations of Italian literature to be issued in bilingual editions, published by the UC Press with a particular kind of scholarly apparatus and critical and historical research in the introductions. I thought that my being absent from Berkeley for two years would probably slow down this project because my colleagues were staying home and I was going to Italy. I discovered, however, that the Italian scholars in literature at the University of Padua were very much interested in English translations of Italian classics; they were interested in new editions of some works or in having already-established Italian editions published in bilingual format and, above all, they were interested in the kind of critical and theoretical research that goes into the introductions to the texts. As a result, the senior professors of the two Italian literature departments at the University of Padua, Vittore Branca and Gianfranco Folena, wishing to underscore the connection between our two universities, joined the editorial board of the series, called Biblioteca Italiana, which has now become a collaborative project and operates on the basis of individual connections. We consult and cooperate in preparing volumes, and if some of us in California have students who plan to work within the framework of this or of a related project, we can send them directly to our Paduan editors and they can send theirs to us. So the Biblioteca Italiana thrives, having grown from a specific need felt first in California that turned out to be something which to colleagues in Padua also seemed important.

I am hopeful that in the future there will be other types of collaborative research like the two examples mentioned above which have specific and defined goals. Certainly all collaborative research should begin with precise content rather than with a formal aim of setting up some collaborative research programs or other. When content is left to be poured in later or is allowed to drain off, the forms of exchanges become merely bureaucratic remains on which hair and fingernails continue to grow but from which life is really gone.

On the other hand, there is no way to keep a good, small idea from growing big. But if such kinds of research equipes and faculty exchanges as those mentioned above can serve as models of the way in which -- even when the plans are huge -- the precision and specificity of the goals can be kept in the foreground, growth can be permitted and limited, alternately as needed, so collaborative research projects will always be moving directly toward concrete goals and will never produce empty forms.

A View from Sweden

Nils N. Stjernquist

In the field of research there is, of course, and there should be, a great deal of competition: competition between scholars, competition between universities, competition between countries -- from many points of view in the same way as in the Olympic Games. That is healthy.

On the other hand, research also presupposes collaboration between scholars, universities, and countries. Whether its fruits be good or bad, the tree of knowledge consists of innumerable grafts contributed by each scholar or group of scholars. Each result must find its right place on the tree of knowledge and that presupposes not only collaboration but also criticism, a dialogue between scholars. The lonely scholar is like the pelican in the wilderness, unable to add to that tree. We are usually talking about the international scientific community and this is what we really need. With a slight modification of a well-known statement we can say: scholars in all countries, unite.

Research today, especially in the field of the sciences, means big money and an armada of people employed. Of the number of scholars who have been active since the beginning of time, more than half are active now. The massive developments in science make it necessary for all countries, except the really large ones, to collaborate with one another.

Ten years ago the Swedish minister of finance asked whether it would not be better for a small country like Sweden to buy the necessary knowledge from abroad than to produce it within the country, thus saving the money which we are investing in research. Our contribution to the total research all over the world does not amount to more than 1 percent. The answer to the question is negative and, as a matter of fact, that was also quite clear to the Minister, when he asked the question. Each country must have something to give to the international scientific community in order to receive something. And each country must have its own scholars who are able to understand and translate the information from abroad and are able to inform their colleagues in other countries. So, within the international scientific community, collaboration is absolutely necessary for small countries. But, in my opinion, it is absolutely necessary for all countries. Sometimes there are people who argue that there is a brain drain taking place from the smaller countries towards the big research centers in the larger countries. That may happen in some cases. However, as far as I can see, the smaller countries would have been in worse situations if the collaboration had not occurred.

Collaboration should not be restricted only to the fields of science and technology. It is just as important for the humanities and the social sciences. Philosophy and history, art and literature deal with facts and values which are inseparable from our living conditions. Psychology, economics, sociology, and political science, all deal with the impact of technological development on society.

The nation-states are an invention of modern time. Earlier there existed in Europe only one empire and one religion. The part of the world which was known was open for everybody and without passport. Craftsmen, businessmen, and tradesmen went from country to country, especially in their younger days, in order to see, to learn, and to build up a network of contacts. So did students and scholars.

The word "university" means a union of teachers and students. When the first universities in medieval times were founded in Europe, they were open to all students from whatever country they might come. The universities were international in a real sense. So in the twelfth and thirteenth centuries students from the Scandinavian countries went to Bologna in Italy in order to get a good education. In the fifteenth century the university in fashion was Paris and, later on, even after the foundation of our own universities, the German and Dutch universities were in vogue.

When my own university, the University of Lund, was founded in 1666, the intention of the Swedish government was to build up a university of brilliant international standards, a *universitas illustrissima*. At that time Sweden belonged to the great powers in Europe. For that reason famous professors, among them Samuel Pufendorf, were recruited from the European continent. The fortunes of war turned, however, and when the university was reopened in 1682 it was as a much poorer university. The standards were no longer international.

The Scandinavian students and scholars continued to go abroad in order to study and learn. One hundred years ago Germany was the center for the scientific world. German was *die Sprache der Wissenschaft* and a great part of the graduate students from the whole world obtained their real training at German or Austrian universities. The accessibility of the German universities was, however, by and large restricted and, to a certain degree, this was already so before 1914. After the Second World War the universities in the United States have taken over the role as centers of the scientific world.

The international scientific community is by definition an open society. The results of fundamental research cannot and must not be secret. The tradition of welcoming foreigners from the era of the great immigration paved the way for the openness of the American universities. At the same time, this tradition has been fruitful for the American universities. The German refugees during the 1930s are a well-known illustration.

Thus, I think I have demonstrated that collaborative research is both necessary and advantageous for all countries. What can we do in order to make it easier for research workers from different countries to come into contact with each other? It is, of course, a question of money. One way, which is at the same time cheap and effective, is faculty exchange. Many of the European university teachers have spent some time in their younger days in the United States. They learned a great deal, established good contacts and made many new friends. A number of the American professors who have studied and taught in Europe have done the same thing. All of this has had an enormous impact. Still, there is among young scholars, at least in the Scandinavian countries, a drive to go west. The exchange is facilitated by different funds and commissions, above all the Fulbright Commission. Why not more of a direct exchange between universities and faculties? I think that Europe and the European universities by and large have been more attractive for American scholars. No longer can there be language problems. Since World War II, English, perhaps with a slight American accent, has become the lingua franca of the scientific community, and at least in northwestern Europe, the "man on the street" usually understands English. You can lecture in your own language everywhere. It is quite obvious that countries like the United Kingdom, France and West Germany are more attractive for American scholars. But also the smaller European democracies, the Benelux countries, and the Scandinavian countries provide much of interest, e.g., in the fields of language and literature, economics and social welfare, politics and government.

For those who stay at home and only at home, it is easy to imagine that one's own country is the center of the world, that they and only they know the right solutions of the problems. But, when one goes abroad, one's perspectives very often and very soon change.

When in the 1270s Marco Polo, the Venetian explorer, came to China, he showed his Chinese host, Khublai Khan, a map of his long trip. China was up in the northeastern corner of the map. Khublai Khan was very irritated. China means the "middle country"; consequently it must be located at the middle of the map. Marco Polo had to remake his map.

A friend of mine, a Swedish businessman, once went by taxi through Mexico City. The driver, a Mexican Indian, stopped at the statue of Columbus and said, "This is Christopher Columbus. He invented America for your convenience but not for ours, because we were here already."

Collaborative research and faculty exchange are useful not only for the progress of research, but also for broadening our perspectives and for helping us to build links between people and between countries, thus promoting better mutual understanding. This is necessary, especially in our time when modern high technology, based on our research work, can afford better opportunities for the survival of mankind. An open international scientific community with well developed collaborative research and faculty exchange is a peace-preserving factor, which should not be underestimated.

D: INTERNATIONAL AND COMPARATIVE STUDIES

The Internationality of Science and the Nationality of Scientists

James S. Coleman

From the outset we might agree that international studies inherently involve comparisons and that comparative studies are inherently international. What I have in mind is comparative cross-national studies and not just comparisons in general.

I would like to focus upon one theme. This is the paradox of the internationality of science and the nationality of scientists.[1] Three points will be made: first, the inherent internationality of science itself; second, the strong strain towards parochialism among scientific practitioners; and third, the falsity of the dichotomy of parochialism and internationalism because both are important. One is reminded of the aphorism, "Every human being is like no other human being, like some other human beings, like all other human beings."

All science, whether hard or soft, is presumptively international in character in that it assumes universality of phenomena. Also, as Robert K. Merton has shown, the normative order which influences the relationships among scientists is internationalist. Their self-identity and their perceptions of how they are judged by their professional peers everywhere reflect the dominant ethos of universalism. So does the norm of communality, the denial of secrecy regarding scientific findings which obligatorily must be universally shared. There is the norm of skepticism; a scientist is skeptical and subjects to critical analysis the results of the research of any scientist anywhere in the interest of universal truth. There is also the norm of disinterestedness. All of these cumulatively nudge scientists to a more universalistic perspective and orientation.

Among social scientists systematic cross-cultural comparison is considered the scientific method. Experimentation is not really available to them. Emile Durkheim argued that comparative sociology as a separate field doesn't really exist; for him, comparative sociology is sociology. Gabriel Almond, pioneer in the great revolution in comparative politics about twenty-five years ago, argued the same for political science.[2] For him, as well, there was not, or should not be, a sub-field of comparative politics and government in the discipline of political science -- the comparative (cross-cultural) study of government and politics is political science. Thus, both Durkheim and Almond stressed that universalism is inherent in their disciplines and that the comparative method was the means by which commonalities, regularities, and universals were established.

The international character of the social scientific enterprise has been reinforced by the special insights of the "outsider." We continue to be amazed by the very precious and rare insight of outsiders like de Tocqueville and Lord Bryce in their descriptions and interpretations of American society. Similarly, it could be argued that Disraeli was really not an Englishman, but an outsider living in England; and for this reason he perceived the reality of England of his day probably more effectively than most others. Again, neither Saint-Simon nor Marx were English, yet they revealed more insight than English analysts of their day into the nature and social consequences of the industrial revolution which England was then pioneering. Here at home, we are reminded of the penetrating analysis of the American race problem in An American Dilemma by the Swede, Gunnar Myrdal[3], and by the seminal contributions to the understanding of American society by a whole generation of gifted immigrants Hitler gave to America. All of these examples illuminate the special insight of the "outsider."

Now, I would like to turn to the second point, the other side of our paradox, namely, the inexorable strain towards the primacy of nationality and parochialism among scientists. Except for the stateless (and, as already observed, some of them have been exceptionally prescient as outsiders) most scientists are born nationals of a particular nation. They are socialized into its culture and its norms which they carry with them for life as part of their inherited baggage. These givens persist despite the continuous pressure of the norms of internationalism. The human tendency everwhere is, of course, to universalize the parochial. Because of the culture-bound nature of their subject matter, social scientists inevitably are more ethnocentric in their paradigms and generalizations than are physical scientists.

The strain towards parochialism among many social scientists is reinforced by their holistic perspective, particularly in political science and anthropology, but also in macro-sociology. The result has been their tendency to neglect the influence of the international environment as a variable in their analysis. This is reflected in the peculiar bifurcation in some prevailing paradigms in the social sciences. Single societies, cultures, or nation-states are studied as isolated wholes; the structure of interaction of these wholes, the international system, is studied as a separate phenomenon; and the nexus or interpenetration between the two is largely neglected. This bifurcation among specialists has reinforced the drift towards parochialism.

And, paradoxically, the larger the scale and the more developed and complex a society, the more parochial and insular its people (including social scientists) tend to become. It can similarly be argued that the more a scientific discipline develops -- as reflected in the greater density of interaction among its practitioners, greater professionalism and greater peer group consciousness and pressure -- the more insular and parochial their practitioners become. This tendency was illuminated by the recommendations of an external review group of leaders from the mainstream of a discipline at the conclusion of their evaluation of a social science department of a major American research university. The external reviewers were highly critical of what they believed to be the excessive emphasis upon international and foreign area studies, arguing that in its own interests and for a higher national standing the department should concentrate upon the mainstream of the discipline, that is, upon American studies.

The peer group "mainstream" pressures in the American social sciences alarmingly accelerate the drift towards cultural closure and insularity. There are obviously countervailing factors, such as this symposium, but the mainstream forces in the disciplines are distressingly parochial. The drift is self-reinforcing because peer groups determine promotions and careers, as professionally they should; nevertheless, they function to reproduce parochialism in each successive generation. And this strain towards insularity is further reinforced by the increasing quantification in the social sciences. Highly sophisticated new mechanisms of quantification and data processing and analysis can technically function only where there is a supportive infrastructure; namely, in the advanced industrial countries of the West. Because such an infrastructure is largely non-existent in the vast reaches of the Third World in which most of humankind lives, the "mainstream" of the disciplines will undoubtedly continue to be disinclined to support more internationalist perspectives.

The postwar global emulation and diffusion of American-generated paradigms, claiming the mantle of universality, has inevitably provoked a reactive nationalism as expressed in the movement towards the nationality of disciplines. There is now serious talk among previously uncritical importers of, for example, a Swedish sociology, a Canadian political science, or an African economics. Kenneth Prewitt, president of the Social Science Research Council, has suggested that there may emerge from this dialectic interaction a new synthesis that is more comprehensively universal. American exporters have been sobered and humbled by the proven inapplicability of their exports and the deflation of their pretentiousness, while the intensity of nationalism among importers has been moderated by the realization that there now can be a common agenda and cooperative quest for universals jointly identified as genuinely universal.[4]

This brings me to my third point. Dichotomies abound in the theorizing and frameworks of analysis of social scientists. In international relations, for example, practitioners and their perspectives have long been categorized as either realist or idealist. One of the currently voguish antinomies is globalism versus regionalism. Globalists are allegedly preoccupied with the spector of the Soviet Union being behind every crisis situation in Third World areas; whereas regionalists argue that such crisis situations are generated solely by local factors and should be dealt with outside Cold War concerns. The reality of many crises is that both regional and global dimensions are, in fact, involved.

The enduring rationale for foreign area studies is the essentiality of comprehending foreign cultures and societies as wholes in all of their distinctive uniqueness. One must have a solid idiographic base in depth, as sought by anthropologists and historians, before one can begin to seek nomothetic generalizations through comparison. This same principle applies to the ongoing argument regarding interdisciplinarity versus unidisciplinarity. Ultimately the most effective interdisciplinarian is a scholar who is solidly rooted in one discipline from which he or she can reach out to other disciplines. The essential point is that the perspective of both poles of most of the dichotomies we use are valid and important, whether the issue is cast in terms of an idiographic versus nomothetic mode of analysis, a realist versus idealist perspective, or a parochial versus internationalist orientation.

NOTES

1. Harry H. Hiller, "Universality of Science and the Question of National Sociologies," American Sociologist 14 (August 1979), pp.425-438.

2. Cited in James S. Coleman and C.R.D. Halisi, "American Political Science and Tropical Africa: Universalism vs. Relativism," The African Studies Review 26 3/4 (September/December 1983), p.40.

3. Gunnar Myrdal, An American Dilemma (New York: Harper and Row, 1962).

4. Kenneth Prewitt, "The Impact of the Developing World on U.S. Social Science Theory and Methodology," in Laurence D. Stifel, Ralph K. Davidson, and James S. Coleman (eds.), Social Sciences and Public Policy in the Developing World (Lexington, MA: D.C. Heath and Company, 1982).

The Chinese University of Hong Kong: Neither Chinese nor British

Choh-Ming Li

In this presentation I wish to place special emphasis on international programs and comparative studies in higher education.

In a country like China, where I was born, we had long experience in international education of a sort. I am referring to the missionary schools, colleges and universities established in China at about the beginning of this century. Christian missionaries from the United States, England, France, and other countries came to China, bringing with them teachers, and sometimes students as well, to work in the educational institutions they established. I was with them from the primary to the university level.

This early experience in international education was not exactly what we mean today by the internationality of higher education because these colleges were established with one single objective: they were, to a heavy extent, religiously oriented. Also, during the first part of this century their concept of higher education was quite different from what it is at the present time. Thus, even though it was the very beginning of education abroad in the broad sense of the term, it constituted only the embryo form of it.

This leads me to a more current time period. Back in 1963 when I was teaching at Berkeley, which I had been doing for many years, I was invited to go to Hong Kong to establish a new university, i.e., The Chinese University of Hong Kong, with a capital "T." This is significant because the Chinese Mainland was then at the height of Mao Tse-tung's power and not long thereafter, in 1966, the Cultural Revolution, which lasted ten years, began.

You may recall that in those days Hong Kong was considered to be an intellectual desert, located beyond the pale of civilization. And the mandate was to set up The Chinese University! After many months of hesitation and resistance I finally yielded and decided to go -- with the encouragement of Dr. Clark Kerr, who was then president of the University of California.

Now, what should one do in tackling such a task? It would have been different if one were to start the university from scratch. But there were already three pre-existing colleges, each with its own board of governors. To organically integrate them into one university was one of the toughest challenges.

The inauguration ceremony took place in early 1964; it was presided over by Her Majesty's representative, the governor of Hong Kong, and attended by community leaders and representatives of many major world universities, including President

Kerr and two or three members of the board of regents of the University of California. In the formal speech I boldly put forward the basic theme of the university in the these words: "The Chinese University of Hong Kong is not going to be a Chinese university (though Hong Kong is 98 percent Chinese), nor is it going to be a British university (though Hong Kong is a British Crown Colony), nor is it going to be an American university (though I come from the United States). It is going to be an international university." I remember very well that the governor of Hong Kong said to me afterwards half-teasingly, "I hope you know what you are doing!"

After this basic philosophy was spelled out, the next step was not so much to explain why higher education must be international, but to answer the question: What are the goals when one affirms that higher education should be international? Without setting forth goals for the faculty, for the students, and for the university (governing) council, one can never achieve that objective. And the goals have to be stated very specifically. How were these goals defined then?

The term "international" may be understood in many ways and, indeed, has been variously defined. But from the standpoint of setting up the goals, I saw two fundamental aspects of the term: on the one hand, it means "worldwide," and on the other, it means "between nations." These twin concepts defined for me the whole program for the new university.

What do I mean by "worldwide"? We all know that there is a world community of universities. There is also the world community of scholarship. And, there is a worldwide academic standard. We must be part of all these if we want to establish a university of some standing.

A question was immediately raised by colleagues at The Chinese University, who are all, needless to say, very well educated, many with doctoral degrees from the top five, ten, or fifteen major universities in the world. They asked, "Mr. Vice Chancellor, how do you define world standards?" I replied:

> That is, indeed, a very difficult subject to deal with. But, let me tell you what I have in mind. The world standard can be defined only in reference to the international recognition given by the world academic community. It is all a matter of recognition. They know you only by the quality of the faculty, the facilities, the research results, and the performance of the graduates. Indeed, all this cannot be quantitatively measured. But, when you visit abroad and identify yourself as coming from The Chinese University of Hong Kong, and the host institution would say, 'Fine! I know your university. Please send us more of your graduates!', then you know where you stand.

For an institution to be so recognized, very high standards must be set for the appointment of faculty members and for the training of students. These, as is well known, are always the key problems for any university administration. What are the devices that have been adopted at The Chinese University to assure itself of such high standards?

The University Ordinance lays down the necessary procedure. For faculty appointment, all posts must be advertised throughout the major countries of the world, especially the United States and the British Commonwealth countries in their professional journals. Those we really want, we contact directly, asking them to apply according to procedure. Then, for each post to be appointed, a panel is set up to assess the qualifications of the applicants. The panel includes one or two internationally known scholars in the field outside the university and several Chinese University faculty members. Thus, it is not just for The Chinese University itself to decide who is the best qualified. On my insistence the University Ordinance provides that no appointment can be made unless the foreign assessor agrees. In the early years, some of the foreign assessors were trying to be helpful by taking a rather condescending attitude, i.e., by sometimes commenting, "For The Chinese University, the candidate is good enough to be appointed." As a result, I made it a practice to say to the external assessor in the letter of invitation, "The criterion by which you render your judgment on the applicant is, 'would you be willing to accept him or her as your colleague in your own university?' That is the criterion I would urge you to adopt."

As to the training of students, the University Ordinance provides for external examiners who serve on the examination committees and who would review the questions prepared by the teaching staff, with the authority to change the questions.

As many of you well know, these arrangements for external assessors and examiners have long been the traditional practice in and among British Commonwealth universities. The Chinese University has only extended the geographical confines to include countries outside the British Commonwealth, especially the United States.

Two other outstanding features of the international system should be mentioned in this connection. The University Ordinance provides for the invitation of outstanding educators from overseas -- two British and two American -- to be members of the university council, the governing body of the institution. Clark Kerr and Lord John Fulton, the founding vice chancellor of Sussex University, have been on the council ever since the beginning, together with, in recent years, Lord Alexander Todd, who not long ago was president of the British Royal Society. At one time or another, President Nathan Pusey of Harvard and President Kingman Brewster of Yale and Sir Cyril Philips, director of the School of Oriental and African Studies at the University of London, also served on the council.

The other feature of The Chinese University of Hong Kong's international system is the setting up of three academic advisory boards on the natural sciences, the humanities, and the social sciences. Each board is composed of world-renowned overseas scholars all of whom are ready to give advice to, and to be consulted by, the university administration.

How has the whole system as outlined above worked? It has worked beautifully. However, I must admit that in the early years some faculty members did complain: "How could you trust foreign experts so much? Couldn't you let us make the final decision?" I had to reply, "I am sorry, but what is required is called for in the University Ordinance."

It is interesting to note that when I talked about all this at some of the world conferences of universities, many of the university presidents from the developing countries raised some common questions by commenting as follows: "You set too high a standard for us. It is too expensive. We cannot afford it. All we are interested in is to educate our people. The university does not need to be first-rate." Such comments have a legitimate economic basis. However, my standard answer was, "If you establish an institution of higher learning without aspiring to attain the world standard, yours is not a university. It will never be a university; it can at best be a college. If you want a real university, you have to aspire to the highest standard, even though its attainment might take you years or forever. Even if you fail, you still have your aspirations to justify the effort of the whole institution. You should aspire to be among the best. I do not say to aspire to be the best -- that would be impossible obviously -- but among the best."

Now let us take up the other concept of "international": namely, "between nations." What I have in mind is cultural exchange for the sake of programming. Professor Burn (Ed. note: Chapter 4) mentioned intellectual borrowing and so forth. I rather prefer the term "cultural exchange."

I am completely convinced that it is extremely important for any educated person both to appreciate the differences between cultures and to respect these differences.

I recall that, again, in the early years, some of the American exchange students who came to The Chinese University complained: "We do things differently at home, so what you are doing here is wrong and no good." I realize that is very natural for some of the young people to feel that way when they are abroad. My answer to them was, "You have to respect the differences between cultures." To respect and appreciate the cultural differences is vital to real international understanding and therefore to international peace.

What is the basic goal of cultural exchange? We talk about cultural exchange all the time, without defining what the goal is. To me, cultural exchange means basically the broadening of the mental horizons of an educated person. In order to do so, there is no substitute for international experience. The Education Abroad Program represents the core of efforts that enables students and faculty members to broaden their horizons. Let me stress that between the two, students and faculty members, it is the latter who must take the lead. That is because the students consciously or unconsciously will rely on the faculty members for guidance. If the faculty members have not broadened their mental horizons, how could you expect the students to do so?

A faculty member may sometimes say, "Well, I am as international as you are. I read the relevant works and write papers on various international subjects." However, to really broaden one's mental horizons, armchair research is not good enough. You must go to live in another culture to acquire actual experience. That is why education abroad is so essential and meaningful. The actual exchange of students and faculty members brings them in contact not only with their counterparts in other cultures, but with the opportunity to really appreciate and respect cultural differences.

For cultural exchange, I have just stressed the important function of broadening the mental horizon. But, latent in cultural exchange is the exciting possibility of pushing the frontiers of human knowledge outwards and upwards. Let me cite some examples.

We all know that over thousands of years China has accumulated data on earthquakes. And yet, the Chinese have not been able to produce a scientifically coherent theory that would encompass all these data. Cultural exchange could promote this kind of scientific endeavor. Imagine, a first-rate seismologist might go to China on exchange, examine all such data with Chinese colleagues, and then come up with some seismological breakthroughs. How else could that be done?

Let me provide another example. This has actually happened at The Chinese University. We all have heard about the Chinese herbs, which the Chinese have used from time immemorial. However, there has been very little scientific analysis of their chemical and medical properties. For instance, there has long been evidence that some of these herbs might be effective for birth control purposes, but no scientific proof has ever been offered. In fact, there had never been a scientific classification of all the different specimens of herbs. To tackle these problems, The Chinese University has operated a research center on Chinese herbs, and many botanists have come to work on the project from abroad. They included one scholar from Harvard. Almost seven years ago the center was recognized by UNESCO as one of the six world centers doing research on native plants for birth control purposes. With such support, the center has been able to collaborate with scientists in the People's Republic of China in identifying and classifying all the herbs. This is the first time in history that such an attempt has been made and represents another possible breakthrough in scientific research.

These two examples -- earthquake data and herbs -- both belong to the natural sciences. What about the social sciences? As Professor Coleman so rightly stressed (Ed. note: Chapter 5), social sciences take society as the frame of reference. Indeed, the social sciences cannot be studied in a vacuum. Of course, there are theorists in different branches of the social sciences. For example, in my field of economics, there is economic theory, which has now become very mathematical, thus inducing many people to think that it has no immediate social reference. But economics without social references is empty. If one talks about economics in the United States without knowing how the Federal Reserve System works and the like, one does not talk sense.

Nevertheless, I am reminded of a statement attributed to John Maynard Keynes, among others, to the effect that theories are engines for thinking. Even for a country like China, which has been operating a very different kind of social and economic system as compared to the United States, these thinking engines will, without a doubt, help a visiting American economist ask the right questions, collect relevant data, and analyze the pertinent problems with scientific rigor. He or she will thus be enabled to contribute something new that would advance the frontiers of knowledge.

Again, some colleagues from the developing countries have raised the question, "You are just too high sounding. We are not trying to broaden the mental horizon of our faculty and students. We are not interested in the sort of cultural exchange you are talking about. Tell us how to give the students a good education." My reply was, "I am sorry, but you are not giving the students a full education. If I may be very frank, your graduates are not well educated." That somehow convinced them.

To accomplish the objective of pushing forward the frontiers of knowledge in the natural and social sciences, The Chinese University has set up three institutes, one on science and technology, another on social studies, and the third on Chinese studies. Each of these institutes runs a number of research centers for comparative studies. In addition, The Chinese University is fortunate to have been associated from the beginning with the University of California's Education Abroad Program. I recall that back in 1963, the day when I was about to accept the invitation from Hong Kong, I telephoned President Kerr for an appointment. His reply was, "You don't need to come to see me, C.M., for I know what you have in mind. The leave of absence you require is agreeable with me." After thanking him for the courtesy, I requested that the Education Abroad Program be extended to The Chinese University as well. He readily acceded to my request.

Part Three

Academic and Cultural Dimensions of Study Abroad

6
The Personal Global Experience

Neil J. Smelser

In his discussion of undergraduate education abroad, Dennis McElrath (Ed. note: Chapter 5) gave us a really crisp little list of things people who studied in Italy on the EAP learned about Italian society. He mentioned the pervasiveness of the political dimension, the centrality of family, and so on. After that, someone in the symposium audience remarked, "Why don't we include this kind of information in orientation meetings with the students so that they will be one step ahead when they begin to study in the host country?" I want to begin by telling you that I tried that and I also want to tell you what happened.

When I was the Education Abroad Program director in the United Kingdom and Ireland for two years, I worked very hard on this orientation speech for the students when they came to London in September. I must say that I developed a really quite refined, I would say almost dazzling, account of British institutions -- and higher education in particular -- as well as an account of what their experiences as students abroad would be like. When I finished, there was a silence. After a time I asked, "Are there any questions?" And then came three or four questions of the following order: "What is the exchange rate between the dollar and the pound today?" and "How do you convert 220 into 110 volts in order to use the hair dryer?"

I learned a lesson from this: While the students listened to my talk, and they heard what I said, they were not in a position really to understand that kind of communication at that moment.

I would like to explore the more personal aspects of the education abroad experience, based both on my own student days abroad as well as my observations while directing some 250 students abroad over a two-year period.

In contemplating this experience of studying abroad, it is helpful to distinguish between the academic, the cultural, and the personal dimensions of that experience. The distinction arises because one is studying <u>something</u>, studying it <u>somewhere else</u> than in one's own culture, and because it is usually an engaging, often exciting, and sometimes disturbing <u>personal</u> experience. But while this distinction can be made, all three aspects blur into one another and, in practice, constitute a kind of global experience, which, if not universal, is sufficiently typical to warrant our describing and understanding it. What I would like to do is to struggle to try to understand and fathom that particular experience.

I will begin, however, somewhere else quite remote from the area of international study, and that is in the world of psychotherapy. At one stage in my career I decided, for better or worse, to undertake training in psychoanalysis. In connection with that training I spent a period of time on the staff in Cowell Hospital on the Berkeley campus, seeing students in a therapeutic setting.

At the beginning of this period, I was under the supervision of a very wise woman, a social worker who had spent a long career as a psychotherapist. On several occasions, she would utter the following sentence to me, "The patient is always wrong." Now, lest you think that this bit of advice was some sadistic variant of psychotherapy, I should explain its meaning immediately. What she meant was that whatever the complaint of the patient, it was a sign that the patient was limited in some way. That is to say, if the patient was tied up with obsessional ritualism, the proper question was, "Why can't this person loosen up?" Or, if the patient flitted about hysterically, "Why couldn't he or she establish more control?" So, you started where the patient was and said, "Something is missing here; what is it that the patient can not do, rather than what is it that the patient is doing."

This is not a bad theory of psychotherapy and I think it is a pretty good theory of education as well. That is to say, it affirms that the student is always wrong. I should explain that as well. The student brings certain predilections, prejudices, and types of knowledge to the education experience and it is up to the teacher to determine what these are and to challenge them, thereby opening up a wider range of possibilities for the student. Thus, if the student is what we call a "straight arrow nut," say a pre-med driven blindly on to medical school, we say, "Put on the brakes, step back. There is more to the educational process than this." We try to press for the larger meanings of the material at hand. If the student is intellectually and politically conservative, the teacher should open radical possibilities. Regarded in this way, education is a kind of limitless, unending process, forever challenging and raising the consciousness of both learner and teacher.

I would argue also that international education is a natural extension of this theory of education. Studying abroad can not fail to be a positively disruptive experience to a student, exposing him or her to new and foreign knowledge, academic styles as well as cultural and personal styles. No matter how good the student may be, no matter how much independence he or she has gained previously by leaving home, the experience of studying in a foreign setting means that the old rules and understandings will not work and that new ways of thinking and learning must be developed.

Let me demonstrate this point by referring to the most difficult case. It has been said that, relatively speaking, it is of more value for a student to study abroad in the humanities, language and literature, or the social sciences, because other societies have distinctively different cultural and academic traditions in these areas. The natural sciences and mathematics by contrast, it is said, do not manifest these differences. To study them abroad adds little, because the learning of them is about the same kind of experience. I would argue that this is untrue, and I can give you an example in support of my view.

Science and math students from the University of California studying in various English universities discover that in math and science, not only is the method of teaching different, but also the conceptual approach is often foreign to them. They discover that in math and science, as in almost everything else, the English are forever asking you to write essays about things. And when they are challenged to write an essay on "the concept of zero" or "the concept of mass" it is a jolting educational experience which they have not had before, having been exposed to problem sets, assignments, lab work, and so on. So, there is a shaking-up experience even in these areas where we think there would be least difference in studying abroad.

In matters of culture, it is easier to demonstrate this principle of the inappropriateness of the old and the need to learn the new. The principle is most obvious when the student is forced to learn and think in a language other than his or her native tongue. Even English proves to be a foreign language in England, Australia, India, and the United States. There are also subtler differences, often experienced, but not often brought into consciousness. Referring again to the case that I know best, the typical British student's friendships tend to be relatively few in number, but quite intense and exclusive. Relationships with those outside the category of "friend" tend to be civil, while on a somewhat superficial plane. American students (I should say California students), who tend to be accustomed to a wider range of fairly open relationships, often complained that they did not get to know any of the natives very well and that they were not well-liked. Such complaints are misdirected in part, because the students are experiencing these feelings in a culture where friendship is understood in terms different from their own. Over time and with wider acquaintance with this pattern, they soon come to take it less seriously and less personally.

Studying abroad for a season is inevitably a deeply moving personal experience, as well. To understand the nature of this, we have to return to psychodynamic considerations once again. Invariably, the experience is a special one, a kind of adventure that evokes moments of intense anticipation in advance, moments of intense euphoria during its course, and moments of painful nostalgia afterwards. Many times, too, it is special in the sense that the student has often been selected in some kind of competition and is, in some sense, a part of a privileged elite for that reason. The emotional underseam of this sense of privilege, of course, is a corresponding sense of guilt for all those who are less privileged back home: brothers and sisters, fellow students, friends. I observed that the most intense personal problems that students abroad brought to me had to do with those occasions of illness or misfortune of loved ones back home. To be sure, these are difficult experiences for anyone to undergo, but when they occur in this context of guilt over having been chosen for a special experience, they become correspondingly magnified and troublesome.

Carrying this line of thinking further, it is possible to point out that -- again, at a kind of subterranean level -- the experience of studying abroad calls for dealing with deep feelings of separation and perhaps even death. It was Freud who observed that the young child does not really distinguish between the death of others and their temporary absence, as when they leave the room, for example. In both cases, the child must deal with the anxieties of separation.

The experience of leaving one's country and spending a period in another always evokes a struggle with feelings of separation, even for those who have long since established their own independence. The experience itself is like a journey that must end; usually it is for a fixed period and the student lives with a certain knowledge that the end is coming. And, at a certain stage in that year, or whatever period it is, a particular sense of desperation comes over the student, that there is only so much time left. It is as though it is a special microcosm of the life course itself; a part of oneself is born at the beginning and a part of oneself dies at the end, and the special period cannot be re-lived, either -- as those who try to do so inevitably discover.

With respect to the transformation of one's feeling towards his or her home culture, there are two commonly voiced views. One is that the student becomes somewhat expatriated from his or her home country and correspondingly positive about the host country. The other, in opposition, is that the student develops more national pride towards his home country and, possibly, hostility towards the host country. Neither of these two versions is true in separation from the other, but both are simultaneously true. Being exposed to difference, one cannot fail to develop more distance from that which is familiar about one's home culture. And, the peculiarities of another culture inevitably have an element of attraction because they constitute a kind of liberating alternative to those rules of the game by which one is asked to live at home. Yet, at the same time, the exposure to difference excites a craving for that which is familiar. The American student abroad will give almost anything for a second-rate taco or hamburger, to say nothing of familiar academic routines.

In addition, those who study abroad inevitably find themselves being criticized and held personally responsible for aspects of their own society which they themselves do not accept. When I was studying abroad in the early 1950s, I was repeatedly asked to stand up and take personal responsibility for Joseph McCarthy and the totalitarian society for which he stood. And, the same applies continuously to criticisms, by those in the host country, of racial oppression and any other evil which can be found in American society and which are seldom accepted by American students themselves who study abroad. The inevitable result of this kind of criticism is an increase in defensiveness and national pride. The truth, then, is that the experience of being and studying abroad generates at least a temporary ambivalence towards both home and host cultures, with stronger positive and stronger critical reactions towards both.

All of this makes the experience of being abroad seem rather confusing and, in fact, it is. Some simplify the confusion by retreating from it, seeking out an island of one's own kind and minimizing that which is foreign. Some others simplify the confusion by embracing it, by going native, by unequivocally clutching that which is foreign, but not really learning from it. The most common outcome, however, according to my experience and observation, is that students in the middle of this confusion typically undergo an experience of significant and sometimes spectacular personal growth. The heretofore uncommitted student may experience a new kind of academic commitment. An important career decision may crystallize. And, certainly students grow with respect to knowledge, tolerance, and cosmopolitanism.

I do not think that we understand this process of growth too well, but it is probable that the student -- jolted by this loss of moorings, this necessary exposure to the foreign -- is temporarily broken down. However, by the same token, that very experience provides a kind of unique opportunity to put it back together. That is what personal growth is about: breaking down the old, incorporating the new, and combining the old and the new into richer and more complex ways of dealing with the world. And as for those undazzled students at my orientation meeting, after their year of study and living, they could give me back my same orientation lecture and really know what it meant.

7
"Marginals" Versus "Centrals"

Ørjar Øyen

A university rector has many opportunities to become educated abroad. It is indeed a great pleasure and an honor for me to visit Santa Barbara for another installment in my education abroad. I admit that there is a lot of anxiety involved in the task of preparing a presentation for such a distinguished audience. But I recall that I felt even greater anxiety when I arrived thirty-two years ago at an airport called Idlewild, my only material property being my pair of skis -- the rest of my luggage having been lost when I changed planes in London. A taxi driver brought my skis and myself to International House in uptown Manhattan on a hot August day. I had heard that taxi drivers ought to be given a tip, and later, after becoming familiar with the coins, I realized that I had given him five cents. He had treated me very nicely and eased my entry into the world of education abroad.

We have a great deal of knowledge about the mobility of students across national boundaries. We have a lot of information available concerning the national origins of foreign students and we know their destinations. We have seen careful analyses of policies relating to the flow of foreign students.[1] We have information enabling us to construct an "international interchange matrix" showing the extent of contact through education abroad between pairs of nations as well as between any particular nation and all other nations. We ought to be in a good position to study features of the interface of nations as reflected through the international mobility of students.[2] In this context, the University of California Education Abroad Program is outstanding with respect to organization, attention to purpose as well as to effect, and concern for the individual student in the Program.

Questions of education abroad become complicated if we wish to explore dimensions which are general in the sense of applying to students coming from any national, educational, cultural background and going to any location in the world. It is even difficult to see the range of academic and cultural dimensions affecting a group of California students in one particular location, be it Bergen or Goettingen or Nairobi. Many studies of education abroad are "single cell studies." They tell us what factors act upon a group of students from A studying in B. But sometimes we would like to derive a general knowledge of the dimensions of education abroad by looking at all cells in the matrix simultaneously.

We must recall that we are dealing with individual students carrying with them their personality characteristics as well as the contextual variables of their home environment, its educational system, its belief systems, and its standards of behavior. In their country of sojourn, they become exposed to a new set of input variables -- the local culture, the features of the educational system -- and while, presumably, some behavioral changes occur in the individual student as a result of the exposure, there are change and diffusion processes going on which may or may not have been evoked, or contributed to, by his or her presence.[3] So, how can we sort out cause and effect in a situation where a vast number of academic and cultural dimensions interact and have mutual effects on one another? It will be understood that in the following I shall attempt to ignore some of these obstacles.

Education abroad is as old as the institution called the "university". Throughout the history of the university we note the rise and decline of centers of higher learning that through contact with foreign students and scholars played a significant role in the diffusion of new knowledge and in rendering science and scholarship international.

Today the mobility of students across national boundaries is recognized not only as having an effect in terms of the international sharing of knowledge; it appears, also, to be a momentous force in the formation and maintenance of networks capable of carrying a wide diversity of content, immaterial as well as material. The carrying capacity resulting from educational exchange may be affected through policy interventions, as has been claimed in the case of Great Britain, where the introduction of a tuition requirement for foreign students seemed to soon bring about a decline in the volume of trade with certain nations, presumably because the contacts created through the presence of certain categories of foreign students in Britain became less frequent.[4]

We know that education abroad is an efficient means of creating bonds of contact, bonds of exchange. But even though we have some indications of the carrying capacity of these bonds and may witness the effects of policy measures upon this carrying capacity, as seen in quasi-social experiments, we have only scattered knowledge about the range of effects in terms of the macro-level interaction between nations and in terms of individual interchange and impact. One approach is that of attempting to analyze the effects of education abroad in relation to the stated _goals_ of education abroad.[5]

What are some of the goals? Why do we wish to promote education abroad? In answering such questions we must keep in mind the interchange matrix to which I have just referred. The interface between one pair of nations contains unique features even when it comes to the formulation of goals for education abroad. And, of course, we will often find clear asymmetry. Partners in exchange, taken as nations, state different goals.

Goals may be empirically determined through the pronouncements made by legislators, university officials, the parents who allow their children to go abroad -- or perhaps reluctantly yield to their urge to go -- and, last but not least, by the students themselves. We realize that there can be no true consensus of goals.

In some countries we are likely to find at least a few politicians who tend to view the investment in education abroad as an efficient, non-military way of means of persuading the others, the foreigners, that "our point of view is the only moral and acceptable point of view." (Military persuasion is perceived by some people as being superior.) Students who are sent abroad are expected to act as political and ideological ambassadors: through contact with our students the people in the host country will come to realize that our way of life leads to a more harmonious and prosperous existence. Obviously, a systematic study of the degree of implementation of such goals would have to deal with the change occurring in the foreigners as a result of their exposure to "our" students. It is perhaps a good thing that such studies face some obstacles, methodologically and otherwise. One effect of stating such goals should not be ignored: it may have a considerable bearing on the funding of education abroad.

On the other hand, we find arguments favoring education abroad as a means of constructing two-way avenues of interchange.[6] The reciprocity of sending students abroad and receiving foreign students in return is presumed to lead to mutual understanding, to broaden the individual's perspectives on life in general, and to create a fabric of mutual respect and to help bring about a pluralistic world or transnational community. Students become links between cultures.[7] Such far-ranging, idealistic objectives must be tempered through a realization that the motivating forces behind the individual student's wish to go abroad sometimes belong to entirely different domains, such as getting away from the reach of parents and having a good time. I am not suggesting that such goals are unacceptable. Many students go abroad to pursue clearly defined scholarly objectives, such as learning another language, or receiving professional training not available at home.

Being deeply involved in promoting educational exchange and in building international university networks, many of us proceed on the assumption that the effects are overwhelmingly positive. At the same time, however, we know that there are serious problems of adaptation affecting the foreign student in ways that are sometimes detrimental to health and to self-conception and that foreign students sometimes are changed so radically that they are culturally, economically, and emotionally incapable of returning to their home countries.

We have noted that we have a considerable lack of goal consensus. I have come to realize that the ambiguity of goals may have some important positive consequences. One such consequence is that goal formulations do not immediately lead to the introduction of particular selection criteria. Thus, we avoid a politization of the selection processes. For example, the ambassadorial persuasion approach to education abroad might, if uniformly accepted, lead to selection criteria differing significantly from selection criteria serving a goal of building reciprocity in cultural influence. So, what I am really stating, is that it is a good thing that our goals are ambiguous. We have no good reason not to select those students who are extremely well integrated in their own culture and who represent no risk of conversion to some other foreign outlook. At the same time, we have no good reason not to select the more non-dogmatic individualists who present a risk that they might return as avid defenders of some "foreign" point of view.

Goals are contradictory in addition to being supplementary. In my opinion, that is an advantage; however, it renders analysis of effect in terms of stated goals a somewhat complicated matter.

We may derive some consolation from the fact that youth often acts against the goals specified by authorities. It has been reported, and maybe this is more of a joke than a verified fact, that Third World parents who wish their sons and daughters to become conservatives send them off to the Patrice Lumumba People's Friendship University in Moscow; however, if they wish their offspring to become radicals and Marxists, they send them to the United States.

At any rate, education abroad is guided by multiple objectives. That is the way it must be. Although we may have scant reason to characterize particular goals as legitimate or illegitimate, we must accept the fact that in national policy, special emphasis will be given to the pursuit of particular goals. It is obvious that a poor country in the Third World is likely to pursue other educational goals than a rich country like the United States. We can therefore not expect symmetry in educational exchange.[8]

Nevertheless, we should be concerned with the different effects of being a foreign student in a foreign land. Keeping the range of goals in mind, I would like to raise a few questions relating to the idea that people have some particular sets of responses enabling different individuals to respond to new cultural experiences in different ways. And I would like to consider the suggestion that being a kind of marginal person in relation to one's own group may have some special merit.

Taking as a point of departure the dimension ranging from the goal of influencing the foreigners on the one hand, to openness to influence by the foreigners on the other, we may delineate the dimensions in terms of which individual students selected for education abroad may show some variation. Such variation could then possibly form one basis for the assessment of differential effects of the sojourn. It is assumed that some individuals tend to respond to strangers through a syndrome called ethnocentrism, while others tend to respond in terms of what we call a cultural relativism approach.

In many studies of the effects of educational exchange, ethnocentrism is taken as an effect variable. There have been several good attempts to assess how a foreign sojourn has changed the student's measures on an ethnocentrism scale. Some studies report effect, but others do not.

There is evidence that people tend, in general, to perceive what they wish to perceive or expect to perceive. There is selective exposure, selective learning, and selective retention; thus, previous attitudes tend to be reinforced rather than changed. Therefore, certain attitudinal response sets already more or less permanently engraved in the personality of the student prior to his departure for education abroad may set the stage for the learning process, the adoption of new insights into the foreign culture, as well as the degree to which he establishes viable bonds of reciprocal contact and influence. Thus, I would like to take certain attitudinal variables as explanatory variables rather than as variables upon which some effect is being recorded. I realize that much can be said against such a position. At any rate I am not making large claims about the permanence and stability of response sets such as ethnocentrism. After all, if I were to reveal one of my own goals for education abroad, I would like more than anything else to see a weakening of the ethnocentric attitude. This issue may have some bearing upon another issue, namely the age, or the educational level, at which the student is sent abroad.

As we know, an ethnocentric person tends to interpret behavior of people in another cultural setting in terms of his own standards of behavior. Deviation from these standards is interpreted as morally wrong and deplorable, although we may often witness a willingness to pardon the deviation by referring to backwardness, a low level of development, and to deficiencies in education and socialization. The ethnocentric person feels that he is right. He is challenged to change the others, to convert them to the proper outlook. The position was amply stated by a distinguished American politician a quarter century ago. He said, dealing with questions of foreign policy: "What we need to say, as American people, and say in unmistakable terms, is that we are right."[9]

At the other extreme we find a statement made on one occasion by Napoleon. After conquering Egypt in 1798 he appeared before the Council of Egyptian Elders that he himself had set up. Draped in the local garb and with a turban wrapped around his head, he declared, "When I am in France I am a Christian, when in Egypt a Mohammedan."[10] It is not that we believe Napoleon; but the position was well-stated.

Teachers of sociology and social anthropology stress the point that cultural relativism should be understood as involving the capacity to view others' behavior in terms of the standards of behavior existing in the minds of the others. The concept of cultural relativism does not imply acceptance, adoption, or submission. It does not presume a pretense of adoption, as in the case of Napoleon. Surely, the practice of cultural relativism may be facilitated by an attitude of empathy, particularly when good social rapport is considered a goal.

My reflection on these questions tells me that I would like to assure an openness of mind and a willingness to question -- I did not say reject -- even some of the more fundamental tenets of the "home" culture, be it from the viewpoint of Norway or the United States. At the same time I realize that if I were to be put in charge of administering criteria for the selection of foreign students coming as visitors to my country, I would wish to have an assurance that they would be fairly well anchored in their own cultural context. This is the ambivalence of my own values. I do believe that many of us would tend to relate differently to a dimension ranging from ethnocentrism to cultural relativism, depending on whether we are at the receiving end or at the sending end.

Obviously, our degree of ethnocentrism versus cultural relativism has some bearing on our loyalty to our own culture and the degree to which we have strong or weak ties to our own group. It seems as though having weak ties to one's own group is an important pre-condition for the ability to relate to other groups. Also, the person who is loosely connected to his own group is more likely than those having strong ties to serve as a mediator of impulses from the outside. In fact, this theme, paradoxical as it may sound, has been referred to as "the strength of weak ties."[11]

This insight comes from research on social diffusion. In social diffusion some item of innovation, be it a new technology or a new idea, or a message or a rumor of some kind, becomes adopted and subsequently spread through a population until some saturation point is reached. A key to the understanding of why some people are more likely than others to become early adopters seems to lie in the network properties which they possess. This is where the distinction between the "marginals" and the "centrals" becomes important.[12] The marginals are particularly useful people. They are the ones who have the weak ties to their own group and, therefore, are more influential in transmitting some item of diffusion into their group. The centrals, the ones with the strong ties, are better at maintaining contact and disseminating information within their group. We see a division of labor. This division of labor may turn out to have some bearing on the permeability of the interface between groups of students, or between a group of students coming from a particular country and the learning environment in which they find themselves during their sojourn. It could well be that the marginals are the most efficient in bringing influences back with them, thus promoting a flow of information across national boundaries. However, for adoption and diffusion to occur, there must be some linkage between marginals and centrals.

When I came as a foreign student to a university in the United States I became a member of an organization called the Cosmopolitan Club ("Cosmo" for short). We engaged in a wide variety of social activities; we produced an international show which we took on the road; we became a close-knit group of friends coming from all over the world; we developed a true collective solidarity.

Of course, American students also were allowed to become members of the Cosmo. It bothered me at the time that the American students who joined and participated were, in many ways, what I perceived to be atypical as Americans. I thought it would have been nice to know the typical representatives of the native student population. I was wrong, of course. The ones we met were, in fact, the marginals, the individuals who could stand with one foot in each camp, so to speak. Their opposites, the centrals, were really inaccessible. They were the gregarious, well-integrated individuals who placed the greatest emphasis on the ties they had to members of their own group; they were more closely tied to their own culture. I am sure I over-simplify the picture when I assert that the marginals played a significant role in mediating between their culture and the variety of cultural backgrounds represented by the foreign students in Cosmo. They were the potential links. There may have been some centrals in the population of foreign students, but, by definition, they would be less active and less visible in the arenas of cross-cultural contact.

I have pointed to the possible existence of a predisposition for people to respond to new cultural stimuli in certain ways. I took ethnocentrism as an illustration of such a predisposition. From there, I went on to a consideration of some network properties of individuals, pointing to the possibility that weak ties may be particularly strong in the sense of serving as bridges between the out-group and the in-group. I'm not so sure it is possible to generalize concerning the research findings on "marginals" versus "centrals," since the results stem from small-scale experimental studies. Yet, I suggest that the general notion of the marginals as being efficient mediators could be useful as a means of understanding some effects of education abroad.

The difference between cultures is sometimes referred to as <u>cultural distance</u>. In exploring effects of ethnocentrism, as well as of marginality, it may be wise to keep in mind that the creation of bonds of reciprocity, and the acceptance of impact, may be more likely when two groups are within a certain range of cultural distance. Beyond this range, that is, when cultural distance is particularly great, impact may neither be sought nor achieved. In some ways the foreign student may find it easier to be <u>very</u> different than being just <u>slightly</u> different.[13]

In universities we are programmed to pay a great deal of attention to scholarly performance. We have designed elaborate ways of measuring the amount of knowledge and to some extent even the reasoning capacity of the students. But, we have no standardized system of measuring degrees of fulfillment of the broader educational goals; we simply assume that somehow the former must be related to the latter and we tend to leave it at that. But this is not so when it comes to educational exchange, to education abroad. It is possible, at least in principle, for students' scholarship accomplishments to be measured and their records of performance transmitted across national boundaries back to their home campuses while they are studying overseas. When we get into difficulties in assessing the effects of education abroad it is because we wish to know a lot more; for example, something about the permeability of cultural boundaries and the role that students can play as mediators between cultures. We are, in fact, subjecting exchange students to a test that goes far beyond what we do to our students in any "home" university. This is the reason why dimensions such as the predisposition to respond to a foreign culture, and marginality in relation to one's own group, appear to be good candidates to serve as explanatory variables.

If scholarly accomplishment were the only objective of education abroad we might favor the advanced and specialized training in a foreign university of some reputation within a particular field. The Norwegian development agency, NORAD, has an extensive program of training advanced students from developing nations, either in their home country, in Norway, or in some third country -- wherever the scholarly effect is considered to be of the greatest value. So, such students become engineers, doctors, dentists, or scientists and they are under contract to serve their home country upon the completion of their study. Such contracts are, obviously, hard to enforce. This program is designed to meet development objectives in Third World countries; as such, it is a very good program.

However, if an important goal of education abroad is to create bonds of inter-personal contacts for students and to acquire an understanding of the other culture and way of life, this may lead to programs that favor the younger and less specialized students. So, at first glance we may have a conflict of interest here. The purely scholarly goals may be best served by learning as much as possible at home and then going abroad for more specialized study. The broader educational goals relating to the permeability of cultural boundaries may be better served by programs of education abroad designed for the younger student. I have tried it both ways. When I went abroad the first time, I was admonished by people who felt I should have taken more advantage of the opportunities at home. But I went; I built networks which have been of great value to me personally, and I know that the bonds of personal contacts that were forged are of great reciprocal value.

Then, a decade later, I set out again as a Ph.D student for an entirely different exposure. I was surrounded by books and blank sheets of paper. I did not even have time to find out whether or not the old Cosmopolitan Club still existed. Although I learned more about my field, I am sure I received less education. The bonds that have remained, and also, the bonds that have had the greatest carrying capacity in terms of my professional interests, are the bonds created during my early period. I am not sure we get more narrow-minded the more advanced and specialized we become; but, there is more focusing of attention and there is less room, less time for multiple exposures. Perhaps we are more sophisticated, we do not marvel at new experiences the way we used to; or do we?

Education abroad is, or ought to be, an emotional experience, emotional in the sense of providing a motivational context for intellectual awareness. I suppose it is good for the student to have acquired a clear conception of some intellectual problem and then, through the experience of education abroad, to be a little shaken by the awareness of the way the problem fits into the interplay of forces in the foreign cultural environment. Striking the proper balance between the intellectual, and academic awareness and specialization on the one hand and the emotional, holistic approach on the other, may seem like a difficult task.[14] I believe that a university's recognition of Pascal's dichotomy between reason and heart -- and the legitimacy of both -- is an important guiding principle in the development of programs for education abroad.

In academe, striving for preeminence is considered to be a valued goal. Elitist performance is highly rewarded. The reward system is linked to something called the hierarchical ordering of universities, in a kind of pecking order. I understand that according to careful assessment based on a wide range of criteria, a certain California institution is judged, for the time being, to be on top.

If we consider our international interchange matrix for a moment, we realize that it contains many features of hierarchical ordering. Studies of the student flow patterns through such a matrix indicate a pecking order. We may assume that students are aware of this pecking order, and we know that there is a belief that a lot of mileage may be gained from having been enrolled in a high-prestige university in a high-prestige country.

I do not wish to suggest that the assumed relationship is entirely spurious. But I would like to post a couple of warnings.

It has been suggested by a transnational Norwegian friend of mine that in building international university networks for student exchange we are, in fact, contributing to building a kind of immaterial, non-territorial continent, a sixth continent.[15] He says that to a very large extent this non-territorial continent becomes a replica of the real world. It contains the same dimensions of power and influence, the same hierarchical ordering and the same pecking order. Such a situation may, in turn, serve to reinforce the structural features which, perhaps, student exchange was envisioned, at least by some of us, to counteract.

In my view, it is important in building bonds through education abroad to be very conscientious in all efforts to secure reciprocity, a true two-way flow. This is, perhaps, one area where students selected for education abroad ought to be made acutely aware -- through a real educational effort -- that they are, in fact, serving a dual task: that of learning from the experience and that of having a positive effect upon the university and the country of their sojourn.

In inter-university cooperation, particularly between universities where there is great disparity in economic conditions, there may be a tendency to view the cooperation as basically an act of charity. Such a view may be shared by both the rich and the poor partner in the cooperative effort. I grant that within many fields of science, the scientific, academic pay-offs in the more restricted sense may not easily yield to a requirement of complete reciprocity. I visited the University of Khartoum in the Sudan some weeks ago. I find it hard to imagine that a Norwegian student or an American student of high-energy physics would be in a particularly favorable position to acquire new knowledge in the laboratory set up there by the Atomic Energy Commission. He might learn that power failures several times a day make it hard to be a physicist.

Yet, one does not need to look very hard to find areas of cooperation where the benefits are obviously mutual: archaeology, history, the life sciences, epidemiology, geology, etc. In some areas one partner has the data; the other has the computer. At any rate, the range of experience is expanded.

There was a time when most principles of sociology were derived from data secured from questionnaires administered to classes of twenty to twenty-four year-old sociology majors in universities in the Midwest of the United States. That was indeed a very good beginning. I suppose some foreign students were there to partake in the questionnaire construction. Since then we have greatly expanded the range of variation in dependent, as well as in independent, variables. We have learned a lot more about the range of conditions under which forms of social behavior occur. But this is a general tendency; it does not apply merely to psychology or sociology, or to social behavior. It is clear to all of us, I am sure, that our encounters with other cultures, through education abroad and through worldwide inter-university cooperation have given us a much improved sense of the context within which academic efforts are pursued. So, let us keep it up.

NOTES

1. For example, see Christine Woesler de Panafieu, Jean-Pierre Jarousse, and Alan Smith, "Foreign Student Flows and Policies in an International Perspective," a Report of the Institute of Education, European Cultural Foundation, Strasbourg, 1981.

2. Ørjar Øyen, "The Integration of Foreign Students," a paper presented at the meeting of the Standing Conference of Rectors, Presidents and Vice-Chancellors of the European Universities (CRE), Grenoble, September 17-18, 1981. Printed in CRE-Information, No. 57 (1982), pp.45-63.

3. In a critical review paper Diether Breitenbach considers such variables and many other complications. See his "A Critique of Interchange Research" (Paper prepared for the annual meeting of the International Society for Educational, Cultural and Scientific Interchanges, Los Angeles, California, March 19-22, 1980).

4. See E.G. Edwards, "Higher Education for Everyone" (Manuscript, 1980) and "The Anatomy of the Academic Melancholy" (Times Higher Educational Supplement, January 11, 1980). Also, see Peter Williams (ed.), The Overseas Student Question: Studies for a Policy (London: Heinemann/Overseas Students Trust, 1981).

5. A review of several studies of effects is given in Deborah Kay Sell, "Research on Attitude Change Among Participants in Foreign Study Experiences" (Paper presented at the annual meeting of the International Studies Association, Philadelphia, March 20, 1981).

6. In his "Educational Exchange Programs: Our Best Foreign Policy Investment," Senator Lowell C. Weicker emphasizes the reciprocity of the exchange: teaching the others, but also learning from the others. See NAFSA Newsletter, Vol. 34, No. 4 (February 1983).

7. See Ingrid Eide, Editor, Students as Links between Cultures (Oslo: Universitetsforlaget, 1970).

8. The existence of such asymmetry has been discussed by Barbara Burn in her contribution to International Role of the Universities in the Eighties (Proceedings of the Michigan State University International Year Conference, April 25-27, 1982), pp. 159-164.

9. Quoted by George A. Lundberg in his "How To Live With People Who Are Wrong," *Can Science Save Us?* 2nd Edition (New York: McKay, 1964).

10. As quoted by Alan Moorehead in *The Blue Nile* (New York: Dell, 1962), p.104.

11. Mark S. Granovetter, "The Strength of Weak Ties," *The American Journal of Sociology* 73, 1973, pp.1360-1380.

12. Gabriel Weiman, "On the Importance of Marginality: One More Step into the Two-Step Flow of Communication," *American Sociological Review* 47, 1982, pp.764-773.

13. Eide, *op.cit.*, 127, 130. See also Ingrid Eide, "Students as Bridges between Cultures" (*Kultura*, Spring 1972).

14. For a discussion of these issues, see John A. Wallace, "Educational Values of Experiential Education," in *Beyond Experience*, edited by Donald Batchelder and Elizabeth G. Warner (Brattleboro, VT: The Experiment Press, 1977).

15. See Johan Galtung, "On the Structure and Function of Transnational Universities," *Prospects* 10, 1980, pp.369-378.

8
Disciplinary Points of View

A: SCIENCE AND TECHNOLOGY

A Paradoxical Challenge
Jorge Fontana

I believe that the science and technology component of undergraduate programs abroad constitutes a particularly challenging aspect of these programs because they present a number of interesting paradoxes. In the first place, the fraction of participants abroad among our undergraduates who are science and technology engineering majors is a small one. I do not know the latest statistics, but I recall that the Education Abroad Program study center which gathers the largest proportionate number of people in that area is the United Kingdom Center, where perhaps a quarter of the UC students are in science and technology. In the other study centers, there is a solid sprinkling, but it really is only a sprinkling. Actually, I would think that not more than perhaps 10 percent of the total number of EAP participants are in science or technology, and most of them in science. Actually, there are very few in engineering.

This constitutes a paradox, coming at a time when everyone is talking about the science and technology gap. We are told that the United States must "shape up" -- that we are doing something wrong because we can no longer compete with foreign countries. On top of that, citing Japan as an example, we are told that some of the differences and things that give her an edge in technology cannot really be acquired except by an early contact with the cultural values of the country. However, very few of our science students go there.

This paradoxical situation is compounded by another one: the science and technology undergraduates on our campuses are probably in closer touch with foreign scholars than those in other areas. That is not an invariable phenomenon, but in the sciences we have plenty of scholars who come from abroad. We have faculty members who are foreign-born, sometimes foreign citizens themselves, and we have a continuous influence of foreign visitors who come to deliver seminars or even stay to give whole courses. However, in spite of the strong foreign influence to which our undergraduates are subjected, they are not generally enthusiastic about going abroad, nor are they interested in learning foreign languages. They would rather be proficient in FORTRAN than in German.

Then, after they graduate, if they continue their studies, they acquire Ph.Ds and get involved professionally in some large company, in a university, or in a research institute. In such capacities they will, very likely, be traveling much more than their counterparts in other fields. They will be going abroad to attend meetings; they will be visiting foreign institutions on leaves of absence that sometimes last for years; they will be on a semi-permanent basis, perhaps, in a number of countries.

How well-prepared are they for working abroad? Certainly they are not as well-prepared as they would have been had they realized in time that outstanding opportunities for overseas study were available.

Why are there so few science and technology participants in the EAP? It is not that the undergraduates in that area are basically different from the others, but that the academic programs they follow do not promote going abroad for a year. Programs in science and technology are highly coordinated. In fact, these programs attempt to accomplish a very difficult task: within a four-year period to produce a competent professional who, along with the necessary specialized preparation, has met the general education requirements which will presumably make him a good member of society.

This task can be achieved only by a highly structured program. Typically, in the third year, when the general education requirements are near completion, most science and engineering departments require a succession of courses which are highly articulated: courses specifically designed to teach the student all that he or she will need to know to take the electives that come in the fourth year. This means that students who go abroad during the third year are deprived of this background. The courses available to them abroad may be excellent, but not courses that will teach them precisely the things that the faculty here at home expect them to know. That creates a difficult situation, particularly for the average science or engineering participant.

For the science or engineering students who do go abroad for study, there is another problem when they return and find that they do not have the same preparation as their peers who remained on their campus. They perhaps know quite a bit more about some things, but not by the approach used by the professor who gave the prerequisite course on their home campus. This is one of the reasons why good academic counseling is so critical for undergraduate programs in these areas.

A student, then, who wants to go abroad as an undergraduate must, in the first place, find out what kind of study program he can follow abroad in order to graduate on schedule. Then -- and this, in my opinion, is unfortunate -- he must convince people in his department and in his college that, indeed, he should go abroad. It does happen that some deans' offices are reluctant to encourage students in the sciences and, even more, in the area of technology, to go abroad. The student is told, "Well, that's fine about the experience that you're going to acquire, but you realize, of course, that it will take you two more quarters to graduate."

Another complication may also arise. Some students, depending on their majors, will go with the best intentions of taking plenty of courses, for instance, in physics, geology and biology. But, as soon as they arrive at the host university, they realize that the advisor who, in most cases, is the director of their study center, may not be well-informed about the availability of courses in that area. This means that these students must seek advice elsewhere. Such advice is sometimes misleading and difficult to interpret by a non-professional. During some of my visits abroad when I was with the UC Education Abroad Program, I found some students who were brilliant but very frustrated. I recall one, in particular, who was a straight A student on one of our home campuses. He was a physics major who had gone to one of the universities in Europe which is known for physics and was looking forward to enriching his education by another approach. He confessed to me that the courses he was taking dealt with material that fell into one of two categories: either what he already knew, or what he could not begin to understand.

This is where another point, alluded to by Neil Smelser (Ed. note: Chapter 6), comes in. It is a mistake to assume that science is the same everywhere. The facts of science are, of course, the same; but the way the teaching is approached is different. What in one place is taught in a certain fashion according to a particular approach is taught completely differently elsewhere. The methodology is not the same. This is a factor which compounds the difficulty of good counseling.

Academic credits are awarded differently in different educational systems. In some systems, academic credits are given on a similar basis as here in the United States; a particular example in this regard is The Hebrew University of Jerusalem. In the American system of higher education, grades are given for courses, students are asked to write essays, and so on. In many universities abroad, this pattern does not prevail. In France, what a student does in a course is important, but only to a certain extent. What counts, as far as graduation requirements are concerned, are certificates. Certificate exams are taken every few years by the students. Thus, an American student in Bordeaux or Montpellier may be amazed that his French colleagues do not seem to do or to worry very much about the courses they are taking. Instead, however, they study hard for these special exams.

Now, I would like to connect some of these scattered thoughts by making a tentative list of topics that may be worth discussing by persons who are involved in the administration of study abroad programs. One is the issue of whether, indeed, science and engineering students are in a substantially different situation than the others. Should these programs be considered afresh? Are there situations in which we must look again at what we are doing, and in which the experience that we have acquired in the context of the humanities, social sciences and so on, is really not fully pertinent in the case of other fields?

A related issue is the program format best suited for students in engineering or science. Should we really go on within the framework of a full year abroad? Or is it best to have another type of program involving a more limited time, say, summers? Should we have a program that comes earlier, or perhaps even later during the four years of undergraduate education? These are all issues to be explored. Then, what should students <u>do</u>

while they are abroad? One possibility is that they should de-emphasize courses in science and technology and concentrate on others.

There is then the issue of coordination between the home campus work and the courses that the student takes abroad. That is basic. We must consider means of preparing the students for the experience abroad, and also the problem of re-entry. When I say "we" there comes a final point: "We" means the university, not only the departments (chemistry, biology) or the Education Abroad Program office. There must a cooperation between these various components of the university. The departments are not necessarily equipped to deal with specialized advising; the Education Abroad Program office certainly is not.

Raising Some Questions

Yoash Vaadia

In this commentary I will address the question of whether, within the Education Abroad Program or similar programs, the study of science and technology by third and fourth year undergraduates in a foreign country should be promoted.

There are different aspects to this question. The first is whether study abroad in a science program is likely to improve the basic scientific training of the student. I think that, in principle, the answer to this question is negative. We can examine this on the basis of simple comparisons. For example, as compared to a complete program at Berkeley (or at Stanford, for that matter) is it preferable to study for an engineering degree at UC Berkeley, transfer to Stanford for the junior year and return to UC for the senior year? The question, I think, makes it clear that in science, changing schools may not be beneficial for the success of the program itself. Different schools have different requirements, different approaches, and different people making decisions. This gives an experience in human diversity, social concepts, and cultural values, but not in the arduous training needed in science and technology.

There is no question that the experience in diversity increases as the distance from Berkeley increases to places across the ocean. The Stanford example, in all likelihood, will require extending the study program for the bachelor's degree by a quarter or two. A similar study program abroad may require at least such an extension, if not longer. In a scientific curriculum, and particularly in a technical one, until the basics are mastered there is a continuation which does not benefit from a change of approach or conceptual outlooks of teaching. We should allow the interchange and the increase of scientific exchange at a level where there is greater scientific content, that is, at the post-graduate level and not at the level of the bachelor degree.

I have a real-life example. The Hebrew University in Jerusalem has probably one of the largest schools for foreign students, nearly two thousand students, all of whom are there by choice, including the thirty-five or so UC students who come under the EAP. It is interesting that in such a large school, in a university that is well-known for its science and technology, there are essentially no foreign students in the program who study science and technology. Students in the sciences do not feel that an undergraduate exchange program is useful for their science.

Are there any advantages to spending a year abroad as an upper-division undergraduate which may compensate for the indicated shortcomings in a science and technology program? This raises the second aspect of the question, which has to do with benefits accruing to individuals and societies when they become more open and less isolated. In this symposium, I have learned that in this context study abroad is more or less accepted as an absolute good. Many learned arguments were presented in support of the benefits associated with cultural exchange. The basis is that exchange promotes familiarity and that understanding reduces fears.

This is my second extended visit to the United States, ten years after my first. It is my impression that the big change in the United States during that period is that it has grown smaller in terms of the perception of the people. Barney Clark became a national hero, and we all care. We all know the weather anywhere in America. The map of America is as familiar as a city road map, and the telephone makes communication as good or better than if we lived in a small village. It used to be a huge America; now it is a small America. It is "television America" by which people can learn more and more about issues and understand them better. This development in America and in the world is due, in part, to scientific exchange and the development of technological means. The exchange of students accelerates the process.

When we want to enlarge the budget of an activity that we think merits an increase, we take all the necessary steps to demonstrate that it is useful. We appoint small working groups that study why the activity is useful, what are the benefits, what are the costs, and why the activity should be promoted. I have not heard that such an evaluation has been carried out in a systematic manner in regard to the value of a year of study abroad by upper-division undergraduate students. If this is true, I recommend that it be done so, particularly in terms of various academic disciplines. In my judgment, the results of such an evaluation would show that the study of science and technology should not be a major reason for an undergraduate to study abroad. However, it is very worthwhile to promote the idea of increasing familiarity between people and the idea of the world as a small village that should live in peace.

B: HUMANITIES

Opening up New Perspectives
Norbert Kamp

The humanities and social sciences compare an especially broad spectrum of issues in international education. This is because they are often concerned with foreign cultures, as well as with differing languages, cultural traditions, and historical developments. Furthermore, these disciplines constitute a field of study with its own particular innate obstacles. For example, as a rule, the only skills that can provide complete access to the phenomena, problems, and themes in question are those that transcend the colloquial language and its means of expression. This applies especially to the field of history and its reference sources, but also to the fields of literature and art. Art, of course, can avail itself of other modes of presentation; namely, those from both diachronic and synchronic viewpoints.

Access to foreign cultures is always dependent on the medium of language which can never be totally compensated for by translation, however highly developed that art may be. Any scholar who seeks an encounter with European history, in the period when its common language was the living Latin of the Middle Ages, and who is thus highly dependent on translation, sees history through the eyes of his grandfather, that is, of the generation which selected the texts that were considered worthy of translation. On the other hand, one cannot close one's eyes to the fact that, even today, famous scholars rely on translations when interpreting humanistic texts with their pupils; therefore, they are still able to illuminate the intellectual values embedded in these texts.

Just as important as the problem of language is a second issue: to a much greater extent than other disciplines, the humanities and social sciences are the children of history. To put it in more concrete terms, they are primarily the children of Romanticism, of the national movements and the historicism of Europe. Philology has thus been viewed in national terms -- often integrated into the reawakening of the national consciousness.

Thus, in broad terms of their contents, structures, forms of thought, and the categories of judgment which are still valid today, history, philology, and the humanities are indebted to their origins in the processes of national self-identification, to the Romantic rediscovery of their own particular historical dimensions, and to the particular forms of life during each historical epoch. Also rooted in these origins are their inner vitality and intellectual wealth which have attracted generation after generation and have communicated lofty educational values to everyone. But, for those outside the national parameters, the origins and the conscious rapprochement of these disciplines with national self-identification, and so forth, meant exclusion, alienation, misunderstanding, and even more. However, if the protective membrane of nationally-defined peculiarities and traditions can be successfully penetrated through a personal encounter with persons and products of another culture, this represents a first category of learning in the augmentation of knowledge in a strange environment. A second category of learning in knowledge development is the special sense of understanding which opens one's consciousness to the roots of another people's self-understanding, culture, historical and literary heritage, and to their intellectual and moral character which have evolved through preceding generations.

The Education Abroad Program's achievement in the humanities which has been obtained in Goettingen must be viewed in the context of such a background. The achievement must also be seen in the light of the wider differences in course structure and pedagogy that exist between our two universities. In California, on the one hand, there is a clear sequence of courses with structured content carried on in classes where discussion is encouraged; on the other hand, in Goettingen, there is an open program of course offerings which may be stimulating, but place heavy demands on students in terms of individual initiative in a less-structured situation. The gap between the systems has been narrowed to a certain degree by the German professors being willing to accept the questions of the California students. These questions are usually in relation to their particular interests and in clearly definable and manageable fields of knowledge. The differences in subject matter, however, have had to be dealt with.

The American students are handicapped in the beginning by an insufficient command of German as well as by gaps in their knowledge that limit both their receptiveness and judgment. Within a few weeks, however, the new environment, which at first had been so unfamiliar, creates an atmosphere that stimulates learning. This provides an energizing climate, as it were, that helps students to overcome psychological barriers in using German, to want to satisfy their cultural and historical curiosities, to learn, and to hasten their readiness to speak and to promote their desire to clarify their problems through informal discussions.

As the day-to-day use of German becomes easier and the enjoyment of discovering something new and different increases, this stimulating climate -- which presupposes mutual openness -- facilitates the establishment of personal contacts more quickly than didactic strategies would lead us to believe.

The differing educational backgrounds of the German and American students would be expected to inhibit class discussion, but this has not been the case. On the contrary, intensive discussion has been achieved because the German side, with a sense of self-assurance in their traditions, based upon their educational background, were stimulated by seemingly obvious questions from the American students to explain things which heretofore had been accepted without question.

I believe that the role played by the humanities in the opening up of new perspectives within the education abroad experience results in the students gaining a new and deeper understanding of history. By this, I mean penetrating not only the sources of past history, but their influence on the various strata of thought, the effects of which can be more readily absorbed when the student is brought into everyday face-to-face contact through teaching and discussion.

The fact that the University of Goettingen was founded by a king of England who was at the time a German prince elector comes at first as a surprise. It then raises questions which again lead on to wider ramifications. More is in store: the plaques on many of the older houses in memory of scholars, poets, and scientists who stayed there during the past 250 years; the atmosphere of idyllic provincial towns still lingering in Goettingen, Goslar or Hannoversch-Munden, with their stately Renaissance houses; the princely residences of Wolfenbuttel and Kassel; the medieval churches and monasteries; and the libraries, also dating from the Middle Ages, with their priceless manuscripts. All of this brings about an awareness of history more intense and profound than any teaching at home could possible convey. This experience more than makes up for the time lost during the first strenuous weeks of following lectures and courses, due to an imperfect knowledge of the language. This highly personal experience with history affords entirely new perspectives and wider horizons to the young student from abroad. At the same time, this experience provides a newly-gained awareness of the historical peculiarities of another country and another people, including their particular political, cultural, and educational traditions. This awareness, that could never be achieved by academic teaching without the temporary immersion in an alien land, helps to breach barriers of misunderstanding.

The matter-of-fact handling of historical material in unfamiliar surroundings, based, of course, on guidance and the gradual acquaintance with facts, enables the student from abroad to transcend the boundaries of national historical self-portraiture, and to discover what is comparable among people and what they have in common. Also, this student is enabled to discover the specific cultural and literary values which can bridge the gap between people much better than might be expected in the face of prejudices that are often due to ignorance and the lack of the particular experiences which only an in-depth study of history can provide.

What I have just outlined with regard to history applies generally to other fields of the humanities as well, especially to German philology and German literary criticism, the long traditions which in Goettingen are associated with names like "Hainbund," Lichtenberg, and the Grimm Brothers. Therefore, I need not repeat myself.

Twenty generations of EAP students have so far studied in Goettingen. In addition to those who for their own reasons made the humanities the focal point of their studies, it was for all of them a very gratifying common experience in international education. Some needed to come for professional reasons (i.e., language); some just wanted to broaden their general knowledge; others wished to become better prepared in technological and economic fields. In meeting these varied demands, the pattern of the program has proved over the years to be quite flexible.

But, in addition to the above, an especially essential benefit of the year abroad seems to me to lie in an extension and deepening of the historical and cultural perspectives for those students who do not intend, primarily, to become historians or philologists. By means of these perspectives the EAP promotes, to a considerable degree, the process of mutual cultural and human understanding among people and communities across frontiers. Above all, it increases the durability of this mutual understanding. This openness for one another certainly involves the Californian students who come to Goettingen -- precisely those in the historical and philological sciences with their specific traditions. However, it also represents a challenge for the German professors and the German students, not only to present the problems and subject matter in a new and different manner, but, above all, to discuss the new questions which are presented to them in new contexts and from perspectives of which they have hitherto not been aware.

C: SOCIAL SCIENCES

Difficulties and Possibilities

S. B. Saul

Social science is a very misunderstood discipline. Certainly, in my own country it is in such bad odor at the moment, to the extent that some of you might know that the secretary of state for education tried to destroy the Social Science Research Council. He made the great mistake of getting advice from Lord Rothschild; in other words, he got advice from someone who owed nothing to anyone, and so got honest advice. The Social Science Research Council survived. Nevertheless, that is not to say that the social sciences are what you would call popular in the public eye.

It seems to me that there are two quite considerable disadvantages for students studying abroad in the social sciences. One relates slightly to what Professor Smelser stated (Ed. note: Chapter 6) in a marvelous phrase, "The student is always wrong," in the sense that whatever his propensities are you must try to give him other options. We do have to admit that there are, particularly in our own field of the social sciences, departments on both sides of the Atlantic in all subjects which are extremely politically biased, and in which the student will not be able adequately to obtain a balanced point of view. He is entitled to another point of view, but he cannot get it. I am not going to suggest that I know how to overcome that, and I am certainly not suggesting political, or any other kind of censorship. But it is a problem, and in a way, it is up to people concerned with the programs to steer students gently away from departments where they are not going to receive the kind of attention that Professor Smelser was advocating.

The other factor which strikes me as particularly difficult in the social sciences is the technicalities and their use in teaching methods. That is not because the technicalities in social science are in any way more difficult than they are in the natural sciences. However, the departments vary enormously in the degree to which they use them. Certainly in Britain you can take students to economics departments where they will find, only in passing, what is actually happening in Britain. Lectures and seminars will be theoretical, mathematical, and econometrical. I am not saying that is a bad thing in itself; nevertheless, some students may not be capable of absorbing what is being provided. I am old-fashioned enough to regret the passing of applied economics as it used to be, where you got a bit of straightforward, factual information about what was going on, and upon which you could base your policy views and analyses. Nevertheless, that does not happen all that much these days and, equally, I must say that I would hesitate to send some of my economic history students to some American universities for very much the same reason: because they seem to be playing elaborate, high-flown technical games rather than trying to answer broad and meaningful issues.

Why, then, do students go abroad and what are the advantages of doing so? One advantage, I suppose, may be that you might be taught by great men. But there are no greater men abroad than there are here, and you are not going to be taught by them in all likelihood if you are an undergraduate. You may be taught something that is special to the country in which you live, but, of course, that applies to many disciplines beyond the social sciences -- languages and literature, for example. Even so, it always strikes me that if you are a student of the Brontes you will not get very much from going to Haworth in Yorkshire on a Sunday afternoon in June. You need to be an extremely determined overseas student and go on a wild, stormy day in February.

The point of going abroad is to better understand the society you are visiting; that is certainly how the students themselves see it when they come back. When I talk to them upon their return, that is what they tell me about -- their experiences in a new country. The courses are usually like the curate's egg; some of them are better in York, some of them worse, and so on. But that is not what really concerns them.

Since the whole purpose of being a social scientist is to do just that -- to understand how a society ticks -- it is extremely valuable to experience another society at first-hand, to study it under guidance, and to make comparisons. It is important to have such an opportunity because social science is an extraordinarily difficult subject -- not, I hasten to say, intellectually difficult in that the conceptual arguments are more difficult to follow and assimilate than in other areas -- but in being based on material that is almost entirely unpredictable in any sense that predictability is understood by the natural sciences. The role of theory, and the leap from theory to practice, is baffling to the stage where many just give up. I know when I was dean of social sciences at Edinburgh, I used to make that point in my initial address to students, because we soon learned that they rapidly became extremely disenchanted. They believed that they had come to a university, that everybody knew the answers, and that suddenly all the curtains would be drawn aside and there the nature of society and the answers would be made clear to them. So I did what I could to persuade them that that was not going to be the case; it was not a popular thing to say, but it was worthwhile.

The study of social science, as far as I am concerned, is not simply an intellectual exercise for its own sake. Of course, that is important, but one hopes that undergraduates will derive from their training something that will be in some way directly relevant and useful, whether they are students graduating and moving outside academic life, or going on to research. I am not saying that training in the social sciences gives the answers -- far from it -- but what I am saying is that it offers the possibility of more natural responses to very complex situations, something more than just the application of common sense. Greater experience overseas should add depth to this capacity to respond intelligently. It seems to me that it is so common in the world at large not to understand the basic nature of the problems social scientists face and not to understand how flexible responses must be. I was thinking of this, for example, in the context of the work of Maynard Keynes, when I was reading a recent symposium about his public life.[1] With his quicksilver mind and his appreciation of the manner in which theoretical ideas should be used, Keynes could change his views quite rapidly in the face of changing circumstances. Politicians may find it difficult to do this because they do not like to be charged with inconsistency, but you will find that Keynes in the middle 1920s was against tariffs, and then by 1930 was in favor of tariffs; he was in favor of devaluation and he was against devaluation; he favored public works in 1930 and was against public works in 1932.

I think it is very important to try to help students cope with the massively difficult problem of understanding the relationship between theory and practice. The most valuable advantage for a student who goes abroad is that he can look at problems in an entirely different context, and this relationship may become much clearer. This does not mean that he will in any real sense come to "understand" that country. Some say that before going abroad students should be taught the values of a country. I have no idea how I would teach an English student the values of Great Britain. I could tell them something about the customs, but I certainly could not tell them what the values are. I think the pitfalls are demonstrated in a recent book by an American scholar who has presumably spent some time in Britain. The book is called, English Culture and the Decline of the Industrial Spirit.[2] I will not go into details, but one thing he does not understand is the British genius for understatement. Secondly, he seems to think that what philosophers, writers, and headmasters of public schools said while living in the balmy non-industrial areas of the South of England, had a marked influence on the thoughts, aspirations and beliefs of industrialists living in Manchester and Glasgow. That really is a nonsensical point of view, but it brings me also to another point related to the year abroad. It is not enough just to stay where you are and believe that by working in Oxford or Cambridge, or York or Exeter, or Canterbury, or any of these lovely places, you are really going to understand very much about English life and values. I am not suggesting that students abroad should be required to study at universities in less desirable locations, but certainly positive efforts should be made to require them to travel, and for the itinerary to depart from the major tourist centers.

To conclude my argument, may I say that if the student in the social sciences is going to make any real use of the year abroad, that year must be geared, above all, to helping him relate the logical framework which is presented to him, to the world in which he lives. But he will not be able to do this on his own without a considerable degree of assistance. The essence of this assistance must not consist of telling him what the values of other people are, because you can feel the values of a country only by experiencing them. Rather, this help must consist of giving him advice on how to go about his studies and making sure that when he comes back, even if you do not exactly examine him on what he has learned, you in some way make clear through the remainder of his course that what he has done is valuable and useful to his whole understanding of what social science is all about.

NOTES

1. D.E. Moggridge, John Maynard Keynes (London: Fontana, 1976).

2. Martin J. Weiner, English Culture and the Decline of the Industrial Spirit (Cambridge and New York: Cambridge University Press, 1981).

The Dilemma of Western Students Studying in the Non-Western World

Joyce K. Kallgren

The role of education abroad for the undergraduate (the typical nineteen or twenty year-old) is to contribute to the overall intellectual growth of the student, by making explicit the gap between the student's culture and experience and that of the visited country. In so doing the student must learn to manage the resulting problems. Thus, I would argue, if one sent a nineteen year-old to Britain, or (with some language capability) to France, Germany, Spain, and related countries, the professor at home would be able to expect that the student (having something of a background simply through exposure to Western culture in high school and the media opportunities available to a university student) would have a foundation, however modest, upon which to build when traveling and living abroad.

However, in the case of the nineteen year-old who goes to study abroad, after two years of Chinese, Japanese, Russian, or other so-called "difficult" languages, the contribution of international education may be more marginal. Why do I argue this? The answer is relatively straightforward and has nothing to do with the intrinsic value of the cultures involved. Rather it has to do with the reasonable expectation of young university students during a ten-month period, dealing with personal growth problems, the niceties of the language that they are studying, and the problems of social values and political choices that they see during their daily lives in the new cultural setting. My argument here is not that there is no value to the year abroad, but rather I am arguing that the value may be more limited and skewed. Therefore, in terms of resource allocations, where the program utilizes the universities' scarce resources, the return may not be worth the investment.

My experience in this matter is limited to service on various committees that select students for travel/study in the People's Republic of China, Hong Kong, and Japan. Many of the smaller American private colleges participate in consortium programs for study in China. Indeed, the University of California participates in what I consider to be the best language program (among a large number of possibilities) for training in China. These programs send their students to a specific campus where the students usually study language, or perhaps the time is divided between language and culture. They are of varied duration, a summer, term or year, and normally conclude with a short trip in the host country. To the extent that the program emphasizes language work, the judgment of success is largely confined to language progress, both oral and written.

For programs that combine more limited language offerings coupled with a modest series of cultural lectures, the effectiveness of the program, indeed its goals, are more difficult to measure, and the result less clear to appraise. The result of this "life" experience for the student is a growth of the understanding of "differences." Students return from these programs reporting on their own experiences with "differences" which are only routinely described in courses and books here. The reality and immediacy of the experience makes it more powerful for the student. The "insights" of these students' experiences often produce lifelong concerns, sometimes professional interests, and certainly ensure the development of citizens more sensitive to differences of life-styles. Occasionally, those insights also include perceptions of political choices and preferences.

Cultural value aside, there is also the matter of "ideology." This relationship between "theory and practice," how to determine and translate cultural preference into work and practical policies, is a more complicated matter. I believe that the capacity of young university students, who have language skills which restrict their access to the workings and communications of a society, to understand the values and administrative choices of the host country and its strengths and weaknesses, is limited. In these difficult areas the maturity, language capability, and social science training of the graduate student are crucial to integrating and analyzing policy implementation.

The issue being raised here is important. What is the field of study for the young university student? Most would readily agree that the science and laboratory courses are more appropriately taken at home. Furthermore, the foreign university is likely to have only limited space and teaching staff. Therefore, both host and visitor can agree that the field is not appropriate for the foreign student.

But what about the social sciences? As Professor Smelser stated (Ed. note: Chapter 6), "It has been said that, relatively speaking, it is of more value for a student to study abroad in the humanities, languages, literatures, or the social sciences because other societies have distinctly different cultural and academic traditions in these areas."

I would agree with the injunction to study the humanities, languages, and literatures, but would not include the social sciences. The reason for this preference was pointed out by Vice Chancellor Saul (Ed. note: in the previous section). He observed that political competence about the visited country requires the capacity to use social science for political purposes. The expectation is that the government will divide resources, and intervene in the life of the citizen. Yet, to understand how this is done, or its consequences for the citizens and their responses to the exercise of government power, all require a language sophistication of the young education abroad student (who is working in the early stages of language ability). Because of his modest language capacity, the student perceives events, interactions, and policies from a limited framework: limited in terms of his or her own personal experience, and limited in terms of the ability to understand the explanation offered by the host country.

One example will illustrate the problem. In 1975-1976 when travel to China was difficult (and not yet as fashionable as it is today) a good friend of mine returned to China. He had lived there in his youth and for a lengthy period in his adult life. When he returned he told me, "You will never realize what tremendous changes the Chinese have made." When I asked him to explain, he used the matter of the awareness of the national language. In China there are a number of major Chinese dialects (complicated by sub-dialects). Thus a citizen from Canton will not understand a compatriot from Peking. Political activists in China since the early part of the twentieth century have tried to broaden the understanding of what is characterized as "the national language," namely the dialect spoken in the Peking area. They hoped that throughout China men and women would gradually learn to speak the "national language" along with their local dialect. Since 1949, the Chinese leadership has emphasized this policy. When my friend returned home to note that "the national language" seemed to be understood in many regions of China, I understood this to mean that the Chinese leadership had been able to broaden the language skills of their population and assist in creating a sense of nationhood through increased communication. Some years after my friend had traveled in China, graduate students in the latter part of their doctoral training traveled to China. None had visited there before. When they returned home, I was anxious to listen to their views. Most of them were admirers of Chairman Mao Tse-tung and hopeful with respect to policy changes in China. One of these visitors said to me, "There is one thing about it. There has been no progress in spreading the national language; everyone speaks a different dialect." What we see in this example is common enough. The visitor who had been a resident in years past observes the progress; the newcomers are inclined to emphasize the limited change. Was the glass half full or half empty?

The lesson from this experience with respect to education abroad for undergraduates has been mentioned by Vice Chancellor Saul. I wish to highlight one aspect: young men and women with limited experience in the world and with only a limited experience in their own culture will, of necessity, be subject to bias in their appraisal. Because political choice, progress, political freedom, dissidence, and similar matters are so intrinsically difficult themselves, I think we should have only the most minimal expectations with respect to the educational contribution study abroad makes to our undergraduate students. In the matter of language and culture, perhaps even history, there is likely to be more success. For politics and economics, it is the graduate student, who is both politically and linguistically more trained, who will have the ability to analyze theory and practice.

To summarize, I have tried to argue the limitations of education abroad in countries where both language and culture are remote from the experience of undergraduate students. I have suggested that in such cases, the contributions of the Education Abroad Program are likely to be primarily, though not exclusively, in the field of languages and, to a lesser degree, in literature and culture. The goal of these caveats is to recognize that the success stories of education abroad are especially pronounced in

Western Europe, where the gap between experience and the foreign culture, while still of importance, is not so vast as to pose a chasm for understanding, where the ability to become competent in the language is a reasonable one during the course of an undergraduate's years, and where the foundation from prior learning provides something of a base on which to build.

In those nations where both culture and language are different and disparate from the experiences of the student, the university should select its students with great care, and give highest preference to the more advanced graduate applicant. Such programs should be small and carefully developed to ensure a solid experience for the limited number of undergraduates competent for such study.

D: LANGUAGE AND CULTURE

The Ultimate Value of Learning a Foreign Language

William M. Brinner

I should like to begin with a couple of very brief comments about remarks made by both Professor Smelser (Ed. note: Chapter 6) and Rector Øyen (Ed. note: Chapter 7). Professor Smelser was very disappointed in students who reacted to his "dazzling orientation" by asking him about the exchange rates and conversion from 220 to 110 volts or the opposite current.

I found in my orientation of EAP students in Jerusalem that it was precisely the students who asked those questions who were the more sophisticated ones. The less sophisticated ones thought that the American dollar worked everywhere in the world, and that you did not need to exchange money. They were unaware that there was more than one current of electricity. It is a matter of looking at these things from very different viewpoints.

Also, let me say in regard to Rector Øyen, who relates the story of Napoleon appearing in Egypt in a turban and Egyptian garb, claiming to be a Muslim while he was in Egypt, that the interesting thing about this story is that it illustrates one of our problems with certain students who go abroad. Napoleon was never accepted as a Muslim by the Egyptians who detested him precisely for his effort of "going native." They knew that he was not a Muslim and that he was not an Egyptian. They would have respected him more had he appeared there as a proud Christian and Frenchman. Somehow, he hit the wrong note.

I happen to be very sensitive to this latter issue right now because I am working on a translation of an Egyptian history of the Napoleonic period. The negative reaction of the Egyptians was to that pretense of having turned native, of being one of "you guys." Sometimes we have to be very sensitive to that aspect of our own self-presentation in a foreign culture and civilization.

Professor Lavroff (Ed. note: Chapter 3) has made reference to the matter of how one language, mainly Latin, helped to make Europe a single cultural area at the time when universities began to arise. This made it possible for scholars to have a universal language of discourse, to travel from place to place, to study at one university in one particular field and at another in a different field. The rise of national states broke up this particular possibility and some of our problems of communication stem from that particular period of the end of universalism. I do not like to mention it, but all of this is seen from a very ethnocentric viewpoint because there was a much larger area of universal civilization that was not mentioned here. In this area, too, scholars traveled from one end of a much larger area to another for a much longer period of time in search of teachers with whom to study. I am talking about the Islamic empire and its successor states.

In the Islamic world, scholars from Afghanistan would travel as far as Spain to seek out a teacher in a particular field with whom they wanted to study. They would then return home and teach his book. The tradition of Islamic scholarship in Arabic during the Middle Ages existed, we must remember, at roughly the same period when the universities in Europe were beginning. Islamic/Arabic scholarship prided itself on its universality.

Arabic-speaking scholars, not necessarily Arabs, could travel for thousands of miles, and did, because we have lists left behind by certain scholars of the mentors with whom they studied. These tell us how far they traveled in order to find wisdom.

There were, therefore, at least two great universes. I do not know enough about the Far East to be able to tell whether something similar existed there. But, we have at least two great universes, each with a common language of scholarship, where people traveled long distances in order to find wisdom wherever it existed.

One of the most interesting features of this period is when Arabic scholarship -- and by Arabic scholarship I mean scholarship in the Arabic language and, again, not necessarily by Arabs -- became known in the West. To a very large extent this was done through the medium of a small group of Jewish scholars who lived in northern Spain and southern France, on the borders between the aforementioned two great universes of scholarship. That is, there were Jewish scholars who knew Arabic and Hebrew and translated Arabic works into Hebrew to make them available to their co-religionists in Europe. Others, who knew Hebrew and Latin, translated those same works from Hebrew into Latin, and eventually made them available to the Christian West.

Therefore, a small group which, because of its size and because of its geographic spread, had to know more than one language, served as a bridge between these two very self-sufficient cultural entities: the Christian/Latin world and the Islamic/Arabic one.

This is the point which I wanted to stress here. We Americans today, speaking a language that is becoming a universal language, or at least we hope it is, are very self-sufficient. By and large, we feel no need to learn to speak or to learn to read what is not available to us (i.e., to speak to those who do not speak our own language or to read what is not available to us in our own language).

We find, in general, as we look at Europe and some of the other countries in which there are EAP study centers, that by and large those countries that had great empires in the past tend to have this same self-sufficient attitude; whereas those countries that were small, limited in area and population, by and large tended to learn more languages in order to be able to converse with the rest of the world.

If we look at the Benelux countries or Scandinavian countries in Europe, or even a country as large as Germany, we find a much greater acceptance of the study of foreign languages than is the case in, let us say, Great Britain, the United States, or France, where the need has not been felt as greatly.

We Americans, not only in this period and not only because of the political situation in our country at this time, have generally been isolationist and insular; we were very content to use our own language, have others learn it and to speak to us if they had anything to say.

What is the point of our learning other languages? Why should we encourage this? Why is it necessary? There are a number of reasons. I would say that one of the experiences that we have when we look at students who participate in the Education Abroad Program, is that those who learn a foreign language tend to have the best experience and come back the most changed. By changed, I do not mean that they have gone native, but that they have experienced some profound maturation in the course of their stay abroad. That is not an argument that would go over in this country, I am afraid. Not everybody feels the need for maturation of this sort or the need to go abroad in order to become a broader person.

When I was young, which was very long ago, I, like most members of my generation, could not dream of travel. At that time, the opportunities for travel that our younger generation of today are able to enjoy, were unthought of. The idea that I would ever get to a foreign country unless there were a war and I was in the army, seemed extremely remote. And so, as a substitute, I studied foreign languages. I studied German, French, and Spanish in high school and then went on to other languages after I entered the university. I did this simply because I thought that this was one way in which I could put myself in touch with other countries, with other cultures. I realize that I was not typical of my generation.

But, I have a son who is now finishing the Berkeley high school system. I find in him a very different approach to foreign language study. He began a number of years ago as what is familiarly called now a "computer freak." This is not an uncommon illness among youngsters of the current generation. From being a computer freak, he became interested in fantasy role-playing games. In some strange way he went on from those two interests to a study of Latin in high school with an inspiring teacher who led him on to the study of classical Greek and his decision now to major in classical languages. This was after an initial rejection of continuing the study of French in the same school.

I think that if we could make the sort of connection between the innate beauty and -- I dislike using this term because it is so old-fashioned -- the logic of language, we could interest many members of our younger generation. This is because it is precisely due to the interest in computers and the concern for computer language, that some youngsters are fascinated as never before by logic.

If we could show, as we should have long ago, that in grammar and syntax every language expresses its own grasp of human logical expression, which in itself is a beautiful thing to study, I think we would be able to interest many more youngsters in the study of foreign languages. Instead, what we do is the opposite. We deaden any interest in foreign language by the very method in which those languages are taught in our high schools, and if we are lucky enough, in our junior high schools. That is, we follow the rote repetition system of pattern sentences with little concern for what makes another language tick. What makes it different from English? And what is even worse, we don't let them know what makes English tick, nor why we speak the way we do. By not doing these things, we have killed any possible interest on the part of our younger generation in the study of languages.

I became very involved in this when I directed the Education Abroad Program in Jerusalem. This is one of the programs for which the Education Abroad Program recommends some foreign language. It is not an absolute requirement because, according to the rules of EAP, if a language is not taught at all of the campuses of the University, it cannot be an absolute requirement that students have that language before being selected for particular programs. Since Hebrew was not taught at all the campuses of the University of California, although it was recommended that students have Hebrew, it could not be required.

I found some of the strangest things happening with students coming to Israel and being required to enroll in the summer intensive program in Hebrew. A variety of reactions occurred. Some did as little as they possibly could get away with, because they felt that if they needed to, they could manage with English. Yet, they boasted at the end of their experience abroad that they were fluent in the language. Fluency to them meant being able to get along in a restaurant on the most elementary level, to know how to ask for the bathroom, to discuss sex, if necessary, and to learn directions. For them, that kind of "fluency" was enough.

To my great dismay, when these students would take advantage of a vacation period to travel in the Mediterranean area or even to go farther afield into Europe and they returned, I would ask them what they did in Europe. They would say, "Oh, I met lots of people." And I would ask if they had been to any cathedrals or museums and so forth. They would say, "Oh, no. We would sit around the cafes. You know it is so interesting to talk to those Europeans." I would ask if they knew any of the languages. "Oh, no. But you can get along." To a very great extent, this, to too many of our students, is a foreign experience. To all too many, it is the way to see the world and to experience other cultures and civilizations.

There were others, however, who took a very different approach. One student from San Diego did not know a word of Hebrew when he came to Jerusalem. He was a very unusual case because he was not a humanist, but wanted to be a physicist. He decided, however, that he was not going to take the easy way out. At the Hebrew University, if you do not know Hebrew, it is possible to take courses in English by prior arrangement with the professors because almost all of the professors, especially in the sciences, are fluent in English. They will, by agreement, give examinations in English at the end of the term. He decided, however, that he was going to take physics in Hebrew. During that summer, he went through all five levels of the intensive language program. This is something that was unheard of. Usually a student starting in Level I would, at the most, end up on Level III by the end of the summer. He completed all five levels and went right into the regular program of physics in Hebrew.

There is no doubt about the fact that it is easier to do physics in Hebrew than it is to do any of the humanities or the social sciences in Hebrew. But this was the extreme opposite to the attitude of, "I can get along."

My question has always been, "Should we in the EAP be more strict in our requirements about language study? Should we be in the forefront of encouraging, and even demanding, greater involvement in language study at the University of California?" Of course, we have a problem. One is a problem that I have mentioned already: not all campuses teach all languages.

We have an even more serious problem, that is, the level at which many of our students are able to use languages at the end of their study, not only in high school, but also at the end of, let us say, two years of study at the university. Again, I shall base my comments on personal experiences. In addition to having been director of the EAP in Jerusalem, I was the director for a number of years of a United States Office of Education program in Cairo for the teaching of Arabic. This program accepted students from across the United States who had completed two years of Arabic study.

We have a big problem in teaching Arabic anywhere in the world, and especially in the United States, in that Arabic is one of the great languages which has built into it a problem of diglossia; that is, two very different levels of language that are used simultaneously: a spoken language and a written language that often are very, very different. Children going to school in an Arabic-speaking environment are really learning a foreign language, although it is called Arabic. This is because the spoken language has no close relationship to the written language.

At Western universities, we teach the written language for the obvious reason that it is the only language the Arabs have in common. The spoken languages differ from area to area, and so, although many universities will teach an Arabic dialect, they cannot hope to teach all of the spoken dialects.

At this program in Cairo, we would get students who fulfilled the requirement of two years of study of Arabic at an American university. But, they almost invariably reached Cairo without knowing how to speak a word of the language. Their reactions, here again, were different and quite remarkable.

There were some who plunged right into the study of the spoken language so that they could get along in the society at the same time that they were improving their study of the written language. There were others who were so taken aback by their lack of ability to be understood or to understand speech after two years of study of the written language that they retreated into a shell and associated only with American or other English-speaking students and made no effort to learn the spoken language.

Our problems, then, are many in regard to the teaching of language. I think they begin from our attitude toward our own language; toward the teaching of English; toward a lack of concern for a standard, for grammar and the like. Teaching at the University of California, which accepts a relatively small percentage of the top students of the high schools of the state, we find students who cannot write a sentence in "proper" English.

Therefore, to begin with, we are faced with the problem of our own language. We then face the problem of attitudes towards foreign languages and that of the lack of adequate instruction in foreign languages. We lack methods of instruction which interest students and help them attain some level of proficiency in those languages.

Why is this important? Why should we be concerned about it? After all, learning foreign languages, as I mentioned previously, is really a luxury in America. We are a self-sufficient culture, a self-sufficient society. Yet, I am very moved by President Saxon's appreciation of the need for educated people to be conversant with the two cultures and the need to break down the barriers between those two cultures (Ed. note: Chapter 1).

Today there is a tremendously great emphasis on the need in our society for science and technology. This is very attractive and it is very easy to sell to politicians. People from as varied backgrounds and points of view as former Governor Brown of California and President Reagan are both enamored of the idea of science and technology as being the way of the future.

We who call ourselves humanists are terribly concerned by a science and a technology that are not accompanied by an appreciation of history, of culture, of the values of human society. Science and technology without these things may destroy civilization. Not that we can guarantee that science and technology accompanied by the values of the past will necessarily go in a different direction, but we would hope that they would.

The learning of languages is not an end in itself. It is not just for the purpose of being able to communicate with others when we go abroad. In order to be able to appreciate human achievement, the ultimate goal of our studies is human civilization, and to value every aspect of the great achievement of human beings over the ages.

We have made our mistakes and we are making them today; we stand in grave danger of making terrible mistakes in the near future. But, we have also accomplished great things. The best way to become aware of what those accomplishments are is through the study of that which is most human: our language. After all, language is the way in which we have communicated and in which we differ from other living creatures.

The study of other languages, as I have stated before, helps us to develop an appreciation for the vast variety of ways in which the human mind has figured out answers to the same problem: How do you get these ideas across? How do you say what you think to someone else?

Without this particular aspect of human culture, I fear that we will be led in the direction of ever greater expenditures on the teaching of science and technology to the exclusion of the humanities. Sometimes I wonder whether the way to sell language and cultural studies to our political leaders would not be to interest them in some gimmicks. They seem to love gimmicks. If it is electronic, it is great.

In Berkeley, for example, we have the Lawrence Hall of Science, a facility created to study the teaching of science and to train teachers of science. I do not know of any facility anywhere in this country where a similar type of research is being done on ways of teaching history, literature, human culture, and human language. Yes, this may be gimmickry. But, maybe what we need is a certain amount of gimmickry, a way of interesting youngsters and not just politicians.

The argument that I am making here is that any way of getting these values across, of arousing interest, and of getting language, literature, and values of human civilization into our educational system and into our students, is better than a general lack of concern for these things which seems to exist to a great extent today. We will better understand our culture through our exposure to other cultures. We will better understand our own language by exposure to other languages. It is as simple as that. It has been said before; it is a truism.

I think the time has come when we have to do something about it. I think as far as EAP is concerned, one of the things we might consider is to have two-tiered programs: one, in which language would not necessarily be a requirement and another, perhaps in the same country, aimed especially at students who do have a good background in the language, with the aim of advancing them even more in their linguistic abilities. However, we would not necessarily have them studying together with the other students.

Perhaps, too, we might have a program specifically for language and culture. The students that I had in Jerusalem, for example, had many different interests. Those who were not necessarily interested in language were very often science students who looked upon the year abroad as a year off from their study of their major. It was almost a lost year. Now, for those students, the experience abroad is one thing. For students with interest in the language, and with at least a good basis in it, the year abroad can be a much richer, a much more varied experience.

I think that EAP should be thinking about this type of two-tiered program in a variety of countries to enable those who have made the effort, to advance even faster towards the goal of achieving some degree of mastery in the language that they have studied. This would represent one small step in which we, as a program, might be involved more deeply in the study and spread of foreign languages and cultures.

Objective and Cognitive Dimensions of Study Abroad

Manfred Stassen

In regard to study abroad, I would like to start from a different point of view of my fellow humanists, and concentrate more on the objective rather than on the subjective dimensions, and more on cognitive than on affective learning. Lastly, I want to mention a few things about the cultural dimension from a somewhat different point of view.

Few people know that Stalin wrote a book on language in which he essentially claimed that language is a dialect with an army.[1] I think this is true. As all of you know, since Latin lost its army when the Roman Empire declined, English replaced it as the lingua franca of science and scholarship.

The linguistic imperialism of English has worked in many countries. This is evident not only in scientific discourse, which is largely conducted in English, but it is also evident in the youth culture. If one travels through Europe it is perfectly possible to hear English pouring out of each and every discotheque. The youth culture, I think, has its own lingua franca and it is English. However, it seems to me that there are cases to be made for the study of more than just that lingua franca of science and of the youth movement. I should like to do this by suggesting two conceptions of language that are important for the understanding of the argument for the study of a foreign language, either before or during a semester within an education abroad program. I will let the experts decide whether these conceptions of language can be made operative in the justification strategies for foreign language acquisition.

One is that language is a "tool," like mathematics. A person who speaks a foreign language is more effective in what he does in a foreign country or in a foreign context at home. This is something that scientists and computer people have always known and that politicians are beginning to understand. This conception of language as a tool is usually easy to sell to someone who has the funds available for language training. At the minimum, language training usually recognizes and caters to the "tool aspect" of language.

But there is more to language and language proficiency than being a tool. Language is also what a German philosopher called a "house," or a city, something you live in. It is a house that has different floors, different rooms; something to which you must accommodate yourself in order to be fully comfortable. A city and a house have certain parts that have grown and expanded gradually; people have built onto them. Some parts are thoroughfares where passage is fairly easy; however, there are also some winding roads. Even in New York, where avenues and streets are numbered, there is the tip of Manhattan where the streets have names, but where orientation is difficult.

There are some people who never even reach the attic of their own house. Needless to say, they have lived in the basement of their own language and, therefore, have no appreciation for the upper stories of someone else's mansion. Yet, we all live in many different houses and in different cities. It seems to me that our world is becoming increasingly a global village, or a global house.

Accordingly, my first point is that it will be absolutely essential in the future for many more people than in the past to know the language on the tool level. It will, however, also be much more important in the future than in the past for many more people to learn the architecture and the interior design, not only of their own language but of other languages as well. This is precisely because we live and must accommodate ourselves to a technological age that has lost national boundaries. It is no longer sufficient to stick to one's own "dialect" and count on one's "army" to make it universally acceptable. The movement towards the "globalization" of the world is accompanied by an equally strong parallel movement towards decentralization, devolution and an emphasis on the cultural identity of minorities, regions, and so forth. Multinational trade organizations and the military need no motivation to go international. They are already there. When NATO representatives gather together, they talk, of course, in English. Usually, they do not talk at a very sophisticated level so they do not need much of it. But, nevertheless, when it comes to multinational trade, the story is a totally different one. Congressman Paul Simon's excellent book, The Tongue-Tied American [2], mentions many instances of fantastic failures in trade ventures because language and cultural differences were not sufficiently understood.

Therefore, at this time let me postulate that most of the world is already bilingual. Even when I travel in the United States, I get the feeling that bilinguality is approaching. It is something that one really does not have to argue for. It is happening despite what people say.

The understanding of language as a "tool," and the understanding of language as a "house" will be necessary in order to guarantee the life-competency for the generations of the twenty-first century. I believe that such understanding will be necessary not only in order to maintain the marketability of education, but will be essential for the survival of humankind.

Thus, I would submit that in order to understand one's own cultural heritage, everyone in the twentieth century -- and this is something for which we educators must prepare -- needs to know his or her mother tongue plus at least one other foreign language. In addition, everyone should learn one other world language, be it Chinese, Japanese, Russian, or Arabic. I think Arabic should be learned, not necessarily for the same reasons cited by Professor Brinner, but for very prosaic reasons. A fourth language is that of computers.

Study abroad is only one way of achieving the goal of mastering at least two foreign languages. But it is not the only way. I think the tool aspect of a foreign language can be learned at home. In fact, before a person is sent abroad in order to live in the house of the foreign language, I would submit that the person be required to know and understand the tool aspect of that language; this would be an absolute necessity for any program that I would run or would support with tax money.

Next, I will turn to the cultural dimensions of study abroad. When it comes to education abroad, particularly when, in regard to graduate students and faculty, one must distinguish between someone who wants to go to Pasadena from someone who wants to go to Cal Tech, to Hamburg, or who wants to go to the electronic syncroton (DESY) that is located there. I have met many people who have been to the electronic syncroton but who have not been to Hamburg. What we are mainly concerned with in this discussion are undergraduates, and the EAP is mostly geared to undergraduates. They usually go to Hamburg. They do not, as yet, have access to the electronic syncroton.

What is the cultural gain of study abroad? Where does the cultural gain _objectively_ lie? Without repeating the familiar arguments about the subjective side of growth and the widening of one's horizon, at least in the same way, it seems to me that the first and foremost cultural dimension of study abroad is a _confrontation_, an awareness of and a struggling with, and, possibly, the eventual overcoming of _prejudice_. Prejudice is a form of judgment; something rational, in a way, which therefore should be taken seriously. The element of prejudice is an important aspect of foreign study abroad. Its recognition as such leads to tangible and immediate concrete results in structuring a program. For instance, it would be very important for educators around the country to recognize that short term programs have been proven to reinforce prejudice. Thus, when plane-loads of critical youths are brought from Europe to this country with the hope that they will become disenchanted with communism through an exposure to the realities of American life -- though this may be an oversimplification, it is something one hears around Washington from time to time -- it should not be surprising if the results are the opposite.

I think that dealing with prejudice is a very important cultural dimension in any kind of study abroad program. However, at the same time, I would like to say that this does not mean that the opposite side of prejudice is uncritical understanding. Also, I believe that one should be, to a certain extent, cautioned against the notion of tolerance. "_Homo sum: humani nihil a me alienum puto_" is an old Latin proverb, in use for over two thousand years, which means, "I am a human and, therefore, nothing human is alien to me." With that kind of an attitude, one can condone a lot of things. In one of Kafka's stories, _The Penal Colony_[3], we meet a researcher who goes to a foreign country in order to study its penal system. He understands it; he understands it perfectly. The scene will be recalled: there is a prisoner who is tortured with a terrible machine and a word is engraved on his chest. He dies before he can decipher the word. The researcher looks on dispassionately as an objective foreign observer, tolerant of strange customs; he understands what is going on, but his understanding does not lead to action. That cannot be the kind of tolerance study abroad should foster.

I would like to make a case for the transformation from prejudice to an informed judgment, on the basis of analysis -- an analysis of one's own previous assumptions. By this I mean the development of a critical mind. A Critique of Pure Tolerance[4] is the title of a book co-authored by Herbert Marcuse, formerly a German professor of philosophy at UC San Diego. (It shows that the University of California system was very tolerant at the time!) This book deals with the theoretical foundation of the distinction between tolerance and critical analysis that I am advancing. I think that culture should be looked upon critically. It should not, as the semiologists try to tell us, be looked upon only as a system of signs. Unfortunately, this is the advice that many people receive who go abroad; they promptly look at the signs: the Germans always shake hands, the Japanese bow, and so forth. I think a foreign culture with its internal logic is not just a system of signs that you must understand, but a system that is open and subjected to critical analysis.

That leads to a reflection, a looking back at one's own home culture, the underlying assumptions of which one would never even think about while living in that culture. Only when that which is normally taken for granted is not present does one actually begin to realize that "something" is missing and that that "something" has an underlying assumption, the existence of which one did not suspect before. The vantage point of a critical knowledge of a foreign culture yields profound insights into one's own culture, which is only then critically "appreciated."

It seems to me that the success of a study abroad year is not necessarily measured by how much someone has assimilated from the host culture. In this country one finds 150 percent-assimilated immigrants everywhere. Some nationals, e.g., the Germans, excel in that more than others. I think that in the context of academic exchanges, which presume the eventual return of the exchangee to his home country, excess assimilation can be, in fact, a deviation and a negative factor.

Also, I think that the study abroad experience is not to be considered successful when somebody has become overly critical. But, it can be measured by the degree of the returnee's political culture, the awareness of his or her own position in and attitude towards one's own society. Professor Øyen (Ed. note: Chapter 7) would call such people who have the ability to look at their own culture from the outside, as it were, the "marginals." Perhaps a successful education abroad program is one that turns the "centrals" into "marginals." What Professor Øyen stated is a beautiful conceptualization of the process I am trying to elucidate.

Finally, and this also has already been mentioned in different connections, an education abroad program is a way of getting to know oneself through the knowledge of the other. Thus, the dimensions of one's personal culture as well as political culture, are greatly enhanced by an education abroad experience.

Lastly, I should mention that through the increasing internationalization of our world, we are experiencing something which Professor John Useem of Michigan State University discovered twenty-five years ago; namely, the development of the so-called "third culture kids." These are people who grow up in two cultures at the same time because they travel around with their academically, diplomatically, or militarily mobile parents who go from one assignment to the next. These people are never really rooted in one culture or another. I think that with the technological advancements, and with increased mobility caused by the internationalization of the world, it might very well be the case that in the twenty-first century we will no longer be worried about acquiring enough knowledge of another culture; nor will we be worried about isolationism. We all, or many of us, might begin to become third culture people anyway.

Study abroad programs, particularly when structured well and mindful of many of the recommendations that have been made throughout the papers in this volume, might be a preparation for us and particularly our children for the time in which they will be third culture people.

NOTES

1. Josef Stalin, Marxism and Linguistics (Moscow, 1950).

2. Paul Simon, The Tongue-Tied American (New York: Continuum Publishing Co., 1980).

3. Franz Kafka, The Penal Colony (New York: Schocken Books, 1948).

4. Robert Paul Wolff, Barrington Moore, Jr. and Herbert Marcuse, A Critique of Pure Tolerance (Boston: Beacon Press, 1969).

Part Four

Sharing Academic Resources: The Ultimate Potential of University Linkage

9
The UCLA Experience with International Programs

Elwin V. Svenson

We at UCLA feel particularly close to the Education Abroad Program, having enjoyed an excellent working relationship with the university-wide administrators and having contributed forty of our faculty to serve as study center directors and two as associate directors. In addition, we are proud of the more than 2,100 students from UCLA who have taken advantage of this outstanding overseas educational opportunity.

While education abroad is central to this discussion (and I personally interviewed and participated in the selection of many of those 2,100 students and have some responsibility for the administration of the EAP on our own campus), my primary experience has been with the international exchange of graduate students and designing programs for faculty.

Perhaps, therefore, I may see this topic from a perspective which is not shared by every educator who participated in the symposium. My experience with foreign programs for over twenty years has led me to the simple proposition that the ultimate potential of international linkage is that which is driven by the academic and professional self-interest of the student, the faculty member, and the institution involved.

In Chile, China, Mexico, Japan, Korea, Yugoslavia, and yes, even Iran, there continues to be clear evidence that the surviving, if not thriving, elements of academic exchange programs are those found in the research that could not have been conducted except for access provided by the exchange of graduate students who pursue their degrees because the opportunity existed for them to maintain research and exposure to ideas through international mobility. By means of this process, the state-of-the-art tools of the academic marketplace are made available to them and the next generation of scholars who are exposed, even minimally, to the opportunities for intellectual development of their forebearers.

Simply stated, one major goal of international academic linkages is to exchange young potential faculty, place them in Ph.D. programs of promise and then return them to their institutions where the results are joint research programs and publications which might never otherwise be seen, let alone read. However, the ultimate goal of such linkages -- although there may be as by-products, some academic "welfarism" or socio-economic development -- is the scholar himself serving his own self interests. Even more briefly stated, it is scholarship.

As was stated in a paper I co-authored in 1980 with Professor James S. Coleman, Director of UCLA's Office of International Studies and Overseas Programs (and I will paraphrase generously), since 1960, the University of California, Los Angeles has established, or is in the process of negotiating, educational links with institutions or organizations in more than twenty-six foreign countries. The majority of these countries are non-Western, developing, and non-democratic. In fact, in regard to the type of political regime, the particular set of countries somewhat reflects the distribution pattern of political systems in the world as it is today: roughly one-third are countries widely considered to engage in serious violations of human rights, from serious to tolerably innocent.

> Given an imperfect world, the determinative consideration has always been: What will enrich and enhance the academic, scientific mission of UCLA scholars and, correlatively, advance as well the universal search for knowledge and truth irrespective of national boundaries?[1]

A major research university has a fundamental and unavoidable responsibility to search aggressively and unceasingly for opportunities and arrangements whereby its scholars can gain access to the fullest range possible of data on the diversities and commonalities of the physical environments and human conditions on our planet -- through systematic comparison and the validation or disconfirmation of propositions generated by scholars regarding one culture or region of the world.

Oppressive regimes are among the most difficult obstacles frustrating the realization of this scientific comparison; however, when scholarly activity is possible, their existence and their practices should not veto the quest for access of meaningful engagement.

Academic linkages have positive serendipitous effects; they can provide scholars and scientific institutions in countries dominated by oppressive regimes with a sense of greater independence and a continuing lifeline to the international fraternity of scholars, pending a return to events which might establish or restore greater freedom. We certainly have seen some of those that occurred in China, from the Cultural Revolution to the current and much more open relationships. Even in our relationships with Chile, I recently had a visit from the first non-military directory of a university in Chile since that military coup. Thus, linkages can serve -- although there are no guarantees that they will -- to nurture liberalizing influences. They provide a means of continuing access not available through other channels.

The imperative that a university should continuously seek linkages with foreign institutions as a means of access for its scholars, as long as, and wherever, meaningful academic work can be conducted, is matched by the imperative that no inter-institutional linkage be sought or established by a university unless it is driven by a solid program of committed faculty.

Without this, there will be no scholarly or scientific product, no sustained institutional engagement, and certainly, no involvement of graduate students.

Because the disservice of academic hucksterism to scholarship is unavoidable, a monitoring mechanism at the highest level must be available to ensure that a genuine constituency within the faculty and among graduate students is being served by a proposed inter-institutional undertaking.

The key operative criteria of the monitoring agency from the beginning must be, "Can we do it effectively?" and "What is in it for us?" The "us" refers to demonstrable faculty and graduate student interest and commitment and competence, and a high potential academic payoff for each institution in the inter-university engagement being reviewed.

Under its Office of International Studies and Overseas Programs, UCLA has been and continues to be significantly involved in a variety of overseas training, research, and exchange programs in collaboration with other academic institutions around the globe. One of the more recent developments has been an extensive exchange program inaugurated with three institutions in the People's Republic of China. We accidentally ended up being the first delegation to the People's Republic of China after the normalization of diplomatic relations. We had been negotiating for a number of years. For more than a year, our trip was postponed. We chose to go on January 1, 1979. This decision was made in November of 1978, and on December fifteenth normalization was announced, so we accidentally ended up entering China as the first United States delegation after normalization.

Also, at the same time, we developed three major exchanges in Indonesia with the Academy of Science, the Ministry of Education and Gadjah Mada University, and with the Import/Export Commission. These programs have proven to be most effective in providing access for our scholars in ways that the United States exchange program has not provided, at least in some instances.

There have been a few disappointments, usually associated with the *force majeure*, as in Iran. However, the net balance has been overwhelmingly positive and productive, as measured by access gained by our faculty and graduate students in situations where such access would otherwise probably have been impossible; a continuous enrichment of the knowledge base on foreign areas in our research, teaching, and our outreach programs; and the overall enhancement of the international dimension of UCLA's academic mission.

To illuminate the enduring principle of the primacy of academic benefits derivable from a linkage, in 1965 the University of California and the University of Chile agreed to establish the *Convenio*, a major program of academic exchange and mutual assistance. Under this formal agreement, each university undertook to recognize the other's courses of study and academic degrees, and to cooperate in the exchange of students and faculty members with the aim of enhancing graduate study and research at both institutions. Funded by the Ford Foundation at a level of approximately $10 million during the years 1965-1978, that linkage came to involve 323 participants from the University of Chile and 287 from the several campuses of the University of California. It included a broad spectrum of programs in agriculture and veterinary medicine, arts and literature, library services and development, natural sciences and engineering, and the social sciences.

The Convenio's operative policy guidelines were to maintain a focus on international standards of academic quality of both programs and participants and a conscious attempt to avoid partisan political considerations in the decision-making process. For the duration of the program, this structure of collaboration worked very effectively within an ethos of strict reciprocal academic benefits, despite dramatic political upheaval.

Beginning in May of 1968 a reform movement swept through the University of Chile, which reflected changes going on in the larger society and, indeed, throughout the world. These reforms, which were subsequently embodied in the new Organic Statute of the university, provided for the abolition of the European chair system, physical reorganization of the university into four major sectors, enlargement of the academic group that votes on academic policies, the granting of some voice to students, and reform of the curriculum and of teaching methods.

During this reform period, the University of California Policy Committee expressed what came to be called its "apolitical" stance which was to become an important guideline in the University of California Policy Committee's relations with the University of Chile under the Convenio in ensuing years.

It was not until 1973, following the military coup which overthrew the Allende government, that the University of California Policy Committee became seriously concerned about the issues of human rights and academic freedom in Chile. The new military junta embarked on a course of direct interference in university affairs to eliminate political activism, especially leftist activity, on the university campuses there.

The February 8, 1974 investigative report by the UC Senate's Policy Committee recommended that despite obvious intrusions into academic freedom, the existing Convenio programs be continued, but that there be a moratorium on new programs or major additions to programs for six months, at which time, if the situation at the University of Chile seemed to be moving in a positive direction, the programs should proceed as before. It was felt that the effect of the Convenio, which supported scholars of varying political viewpoints, was beneficial, and that continued academic collaboration between the two universities would most likely have a positive influence with respect to academic freedom.

The implementation of this policy produced a bifurcated situation. In the general areas of agriculture, science and engineering, the elimination of political activism, in fact, created a situation in which more teaching, research, and pluralistic publications could proceed more efficiently than previously. On the other hand, the purge of dissident faculty in the social sciences and certain professional areas of the university left these areas dramatically affected in the reverse sense. The exchange program entered a new phase of reduced activity which facilitated the working together of scholars and allowed Chilean students in all fields already enrolled in the University of California to continue and complete their degree programs.

This new phase was soon interrupted by further events in Chile: a Chilean professor who had been involved in the Convenio disappeared. At the same time, on political grounds, the government explicitly ordered the immediate return of a Chilean student who was pursuing a Ph.D. degree under the Convenio auspices at the University of California, Santa Barbara.

The University of California demanded answers to allegations of unacceptable political pressure and activity and a proposed visit of an academic delegation was canceled. A week later the civilian protector of the University of Chile explained by telex that the missing professor had been arrested by the government, and that the UC Santa Barbara graduate student was authorized to remain there to complete his studies. This reply satisfied the UC Senate Policy Committee, which recognized that the case of the professor was _sub judice_, an internal Chilean affair about which the University of Chile could do very little. (It should be noted that the professor concerned was not prosecuted and was ultimately allowed to leave Chile to accept a teaching position in Venezuela, a situation in which our direct involvement in negotiations produced a positive result.) A postponed visit of a California professor to Chile was rescheduled and the previously established reduced level of activity was resumed.

From 1973 through most of 1975 many University of California faculty members and students advocated the termination of the Convenio or attempted to capitalize on its existence as a means of applying pressure on the Chilean government to moderate its policies. However, the chairman of the University Senate Committee on Academic Freedom urged that the Convenio not be terminated, but rather used as a lever to help Chilean scholars as necessary through negotiations maintained exclusively with University officials. The chairman of the UC Senate Policy Committee wrote on February 24, 1975:

> ...the University of California entered into this agreement as a party in a cooperative relationship with another academic institution and for the purpose of furthering the academic objectives of the two participating institutions, irrespective of governments. The Committee concedes that its basic, apolitical role has not been easily maintained through the years; however, having survived the turbulence of the Frei and Allende administrations and one year and a half of the present military regime, we consider that one of the program's successful features has been its relative ability to stay above Chilean politics.[2]

The University of California Academic Senate supported the views of the Convenio Policy Committee when, on May 29, 1975, it voted against the motion to abrogate the Convenio, while allowing Chilean graduate students at the University of California under the program to continue their studies with funding from the Ford Foundation and other sources. Thus, the Convenio was maintained without modification until July, 1976. By then the Ford Foundation support had terminated as originally envisaged. However, as the Convenio itself was of indefinite duration, a new agreement was signed in July, 1976 between the two universities, encouraging individual scholars to continue collaboration on a one-to-one basis. Since 1976 we have had from seven to twenty of our faculty from several campuses continue their research with their former graduate students or develop new programs.

The other cooperative program in which the issue of human rights and academic freedom arose was with an Iranian institution. Beginning in 1975, linkage was established between UCLA and the University of Teacher Education (UTE) in Teheran, Iran. The linkage was for the purpose of developing UTE's graduate programs, upgrading its faculty, and developing new faculty for UTE, while providing UCLA faculty with opportunities for research. The program was funded entirely by UTE.

In March, 1976, the issue of political repression in Iran came up at a UCLA review meeting. Some of the UCLA faculty who opposed involvement in Iran expressed their concern over the effect this repression had on human rights and academic freedom. The issue was thoroughly discussed. It was resolved that while each individual faculty member had to reach his or her own decision on this matter, UCLA, as an institution, would take a clear and unequivocal stance in support of the academic freedom of all faculty and students from both universities. Although this position was never tested, UCLA intended to withdraw from the relationship if any incidents occurred to threaten the academic freedom of those faculty and graduate students involved. It was probably the principle of academic freedom that enabled the entire project to go forward: once those who felt the UCLA-UTE program was inappropriate had made their statement and participated in the debate, they were willing to let others, who found the relationship productive, or potentially productive, to proceed. In mid-1979, the Iranian Revolution, however, cut off further funds and brought the program to a halt before all of its objectives could be realized. There was, however, a program where, in accordance with our contractual agreements, we had managed to accumulate about $800 million which allowed all the Iranian students, as well as some other students, to complete the degrees that they had planned. The final funds were spent in two months. This is the only university that I know of that had money to survive the interruptions in programs resulting from the Iranian revolution.

The principles and guidelines which have governed UCLA's engagement in foreign programs, some held a priori and others derived from its varied experiences, can be summarized as follows:

1. In weighing the pros and cons of involvement in an academic exchange program or other type of educational relationship with an institution in a foreign country, the chief considerations should be the academic merit, feasibility, and viability of the proposed undertaking, including, particularly, the access and academic benefits accruing to one's own faculty and graduate students.

2. The danger that the existence of a linkage with a university in a foreign country ipso facto functions to legitimize and strengthen its repressive government is far outweighed by the likelihood -- indeed, the demonstrable fact -- that the relationship can operate to nurture and further a sense of identity with the international fraternity of scholars committed to the search for

knowledge and scientific objectivity as well as enhance access for research. The seemingly illogical phenomenon of "permissive authoritarianism" in which human rights may be curtailed, but the islands of academic freedom may still exist, should be recognized as part of reality in many countries of the world today. (There are two classic illustrations of this. One of our faculty had a United States grant to study in China. He was not given access to the library that he wanted to use until UCLA had negotiated an agreement which was bilateral between the two institutions. The second is Indiana University's current program in Poland where the government is allowing it to continue and urging a much higher freedom of academic and scholarly exchange than exists in other parts of that country.)

3. The relationship between the universities should, to the maximum extent possible, be bilateral. The uniquely precious nature of the university-to-university linkage not only facilitates access but enables many things to be done that otherwise could not be done. It serves to preserve the quintessentially academic and apolitical nature of the relationship.

4. Each foreign undertaking should be considered on an ad hoc basis. UCLA has had no predetermined criteria by which it judges a proposal for an overseas linkage other than those already mentioned, plus certain university-wide regulations covering such matters as contract and grant requirements, patents and copyright, protection of human subjects in research, and the like.

5. The criterion for termination of a program is clear, namely, termination is initiated when meaningful academic work can no longer be conducted, for whatever reason.

6. Validating, monitoring, and oversight structures at the highest university-wide level, with broadly-based faculty representation, are indispensable to ensure: a) that any foreign undertaking is based solidly upon the interests and competence, and a capacity to consummate, of a cluster of faculty and graduate students whose professional and scientific work will be furthered; b) that it conforms to all university criteria governing overseas commitments; and c) that throughout its life it continues to be a productive and mutually beneficial relationship.

7. The university, as such, should not take an open public institutional position regarding the actions of a foreign government or the nature of its regime; individual scholars should be encouraged to state publicly their own individual positions as forcefully as they wish, but not as spokespersons for the university. Universities should, however, take a firm stand as regards any issue that affects the conditions necessary for their scholars to carry out their professional work. In these areas the university has a moral responsibility to ensure that the requisite conditions are not infringed or denied.

In all instances, though principle may be tested, philosophy challenged, and cultural or political sensitivities shocked, we continue to labor to maintain this vision of the ultimate potential of university linkage throughout the world when academics work together on an equal basis with the single-minded purpose of advancing human relationships and extending scholarly activities.

NOTES

1. "UCLA Experience with Foreign Programs," Human Rights Quarterly, February 1984 (Johns Hopkins University Press), pp.56-57.

2. From a letter dated February 24, 1975, page 2, by Charles E. Young, Chairman of the UC Senate Policy Committee, to Professor Stanley V. Anderson.

10
Prospects for Sharing

Sir Kenneth Alexander

Educationists feel comfortable discussing ultimates, for who can deny that Mark Twain had it right when he stated: "Soap and education are not as sudden as a massacre, but they are more deadly in the long run."[1] Threatening appraisals of policy and performance over short time-spans can be deflected by reference to the ultimate (long-run) benefits, but the ultimate never comes. Being far from home and out of range, I propose to deny myself the protection of that word, "ultimate"; after all, there is still a good deal of protection in "potential."

What are the academic resources which can be shared? I see three categories, overlapping to a considerable extent. The first category is institutional: the universities and colleges, their libraries, laboratories, and departmental strengths (including institutes, units, etc.).

The second category consists of individuals: faculty members as teachers and researchers and other staff members with special skills.

The third category consists of areas of research: a university may, either by sustained effort or by good fortune (e.g., geographical location), have a favored and privileged position in relation to particular areas of research.

Do we need to make a case for sharing? I think we do because among those involved in educational exchange some have cast doubt on sharing at all, particularly at the undergraduate level. Why does even as large, heterogeneous, and prestigious a university as the University of California attach enough importance to such sharing as to have convened this symposium to consider this matter?

The case for sharing has three dimensions. Barbara Burn (Ed. note: Chapter 4) suggested five; I believe my three cover the same areas. The first relates to the needs of particular universities, the second to the pursuit of scholarship in the widest sense, and the third to objectives beyond scholarship -- in the economic sphere or the sphere of international relations. Although a great deal can be said about this third dimension, I intend to let it speak for itself. The involvement of national governments in encouraging the sharing of resources (subsidizing academic travel and foreign students, etc.) reflects an appreciation by government of the importance of this third dimension, and perhaps a recognition that subsidization is required if these gains which are external to the universities are to be achieved at the desired level. The case which produced the recent mini-U-turn by the British government, relaxing its earlier policy of full-cost fees for all non-EEC students, provides some evidence of this. Another initiative, international and with great potential, is currently being incubated ready to be hatched at the economic summit conference in May, 1983. There are eighteen cooperative research projects in view, with a working group of government scientists from the seven summit nations and the European community charged with producing specific proposals for consideration by the presidents and prime ministers.

What interests me about this is that in what is essentially a scholarly activity, the initiative has not come from the scholars, but from the prime ministers and presidents, and their civil servants. However, the degree of impact which scholars, per se, can have on this initiative is considerably limited by the fact that they played no part in choosing, for example, the eighteen areas.

(Ed. note: Readers who wish to have more information concerning directives, resolutions, and conclusions on education adopted at the European Community level are referred to European Educational Policy Statements 1974-1983 and other publications of the Council of the European Communities, Office for Official Publications of the European Communities, L-2985, Luxembourg.)

There are not many disadvantages to the sharing of academic resources. But, account should be taken of the subverting effects that can trouble an autocratic government or the unsettling effects that can cause concern for the senior staff of a poor university which sees its young hopefuls who are on temporary assignment to a more generously funded institution. Thus, in spite of the fact that there are few disadvantages, it seems appropriate to give some attention to the many obstacles and difficulties connected with the sharing of academic resources before turning to the potential. If, as I believe, present practice falls short of what is possible and desirable, let us consider some of these from the perspective of positive steps that can be taken.

May I begin by mentioning the impact of technological change. Libraries can be and are shared. An understanding of equipment can be facilitated without long-distance traveling when description and diagrams can be explained by a video presentation of the equipment in use. By the simple device of a telephone link between two data processing systems, data bases can now be drawn upon across great distances. Similarly, discussions between widely separated groups of scholars can be brought to life with the aid of television. Already the use of teaching materials produced by Britain's Open University (OU), such as audio and video tapes with supporting texts, are being used quite widely in other countries, and no doubt there are other examples of such transfers.

The international impact of Britain's Open University is very extensive and worth consideration as a model which could be developed more widely by other university systems. It has helped the extension of distance-learning universities in seven countries, with two other countries now in process. In addition, individual faculty members of the Open University have helped in seven other countries in a private capacity. In the United States, three universities were interested in utilizing OU materials. As a result, an American office was established through the British Open University Foundation from which has developed the National Universities Consortium in Maryland. This consortium sends out materials to a number of American universities, some twenty in all. In this connection, the Vice Chancellor of the Open University has stated as follows:

> The American example best illustrates the difficulties of exporting the British Open University system to another country. The Open University is based on four main planks. Firstly, cooperation with a very closely integrated higher education system, using tutors from many other universities, many polytechnics and many institutes of education.
>
> Secondly, we are able to recruit so many students because the UK system of primary and secondary education is really pretty good in spite of the criticism it is subjected to. It means that people who have not obtained university entry have got a base on which they can build subsequently with the Open University.
>
> Thirdly, there is the essential point that our age participation rate -- the number of eighteen year-olds which go through to higher education is relatively small in comparison with other western countries. Unfortunately, it is decreasing further and we do really seem to be unable to get this across to the nation as a whole. Our age participation rate at 12 percent is near the bottom of the league in Europe and yet people still talk about too many people going to universities. It is quite incredible to me.
>
> The fourth and final point is the cooperation with the BBC -- a national radio and television network -- and the tremendous benefit that the Open University has had from that partnership. Such an arrangement doesn't really exist in America and is one of the reasons why the OU system has not yet blossomed there.[2]

The OU has other international activities of note. A separate company, Open University Educational Enterprises, is wholly owned by the OU and markets its materials to non-students. The company's turnover is about $2.25 million per year. The University translates courses into other languages and makes these available for sale. Open University teaching has contributions from overseas academics; for example, academics at the University of California collaborate in a course called, "Understanding Space and Time."

The Open University has an international documentation center which collects and holds information on distance learning in over eighty countries around the world.

It seems that information technology will provide many opportunities for sharing which are not yet possible, and perhaps not yet conceivable. However, the movement of people -- students and staff -- remains and will remain an essential element in the sharing of institutional resources and of faculty members. This brings us up against the cost difficulties; even after the most welcome resurgence of competition between travel operators, it is still expensive to move people from country to country. In most cases, the shorter the visit, the higher the cost-to-benefit ratio, and the longer the visit, the more difficult it is to arrange, because of the disruption to learning or teaching in the home university. The manner in which the universities themselves grapple with the disruption obstacle provides a test of what value they attach to the exchanges which longer visits would encourage. Initial contacts are necessary to unravel the different modes of teaching, ordering and time-tabling of subject matter, range and depth of specialist teaching, etc., but once the fact-finding is over, the more testing tasks of change must be faced. If difficulties are to be overcome, it is vital that universities have powerful committees responsible for and committed to overseas links and capable of making the case for changes which will make these easier to facilitate. Such committees must have powerful support from the top administration. This requirement applies across the board, and not only to student and staff exchanges. An effective focus within each university -- influential and administratively efficient -- is a necessary condition if linkages, exchanges, and sharing are to be developed.

Undergraduates, postgraduates, or faculty -- which flow yields the best return? The issue must be faced as long as the resources available to make movement possible are in very short supply. Both the costs and benefits can differ according to the circumstances. Even when the cost to each is broadly the same, a poor university in the Third World may require a more certain and higher benefit than a richer university. If the benefits to scholarship in general and/or to the nation in commercial terms (technology transfer or long-term goodwill) are included in the calculation, and matching subsidy provided, then the university(ies) making the decision to share resources or faculty will increase the quantities to be shared. The assessment of benefits, in particular, is complicated by the fact that these are shared by the university and the person who moves, but "belong" to the latter.

When looking at the choice between undergraduates, postgraduates, and faculty, we heard from Rector Øyen (Ed. note: Chapter 7) that the benefits to an undergraduate, enjoying the benefits of cultural exchange, would possibly be greater and last longer, because at an earlier stage in life, the undergraduate is able to absorb more and benefit more from the experience of an exchange.

The lead-in time before benefits can flow is longest for undergraduate exchanges, and this must be a deterrent to the establishment and extension of such programs, or at least to the substantial subsidy of such programs. Exchange programs reduce the costs, but cannot affect the time-scale. In some subjects, for example, modern languages and archaeology, the benefit may be close to a necessity if the undergraduate course is to be adequate. In other subjects, it may be a major advantage, filling gaps or achieving standards which cannot be met by the home university. The ready response made by the University of California to the University of Stirling's suggestion that our undergraduate physicists spend year three of a four-year honors course at UC

Santa Barbara has made it possible for our course to survive, and to survive in a strengthened form. The University of East Anglia's chemistry degree program benefits from a similar arrangement with the University of Massachusetts. Various programs in UK universities integrate a semester or full year with European universities. In other cases, movement across national boundaries may bring no specific academic benefits, although the more general benefit of a "broadening experience" can be claimed in almost every case. The most ambitious and effective developments have come from the United States, with its happy combination of open-minded academic internationalism and the per capita GNP to encourage it. Professor Dahrendorf (Ed. note: Chapter 2) questioned whether the United States, as a nation, is sufficiently internationalistic; as an academic community I believe that it certainly passes the test. Those universities and campuses which incorporate a year abroad study program not only do well by their students, but make an important contribution to the academic, cultural, and social life of the receiving universities.

A fortnight ago I met with ten of our undergraduates who spent a semester last year at a number of universities in America. We talked for an hour or so, and not one doubt was expressed about the worthwhileness of the experience. Indeed, the point was made very forcibly that quite possibly a few, at least, had lost grades as a result and would finish at Stirling with a degree classification lower than had they stayed at home, but that the overall experience would more than compensate for such an outcome. Specific comments which seemed to represent the views of the group included the following:

a) The impact on the perception of one's own country is even greater than on the perception of the USA, but, the idea of a stereotyped American is abandoned in the face of experience;

b) American universities put more emphasis on technical expertise (e.g., in accountancy, management science) and less on "depth" and "breadth" than at Stirling; and

c) American students are less keen on political discussion than are British students (the Stirling students had been in the United States during the Falkland Islands crisis and found this event a route to political discussion with their American colleagues).

Comments as to how the visits could be made more successful included the following, which appeared to have majority support:

a) Additional, and more up-to-date, information is needed about the courses the visiting students are to take;

b) More advice is required from the receiving university once the student has arrived; and

c) A thorough de-briefing should take place when a student returns to his or her home campus, partly in the interests of the individual student and partly as a way to build up more effective and more up-to-date information about the universities visited.

The movement of postgraduates is quite different. They go from one nation to the university of another in most cases without any formal institutional academic base in the home country. The period of absence will usually be longer and the academic work more specialized and advanced. Most of the benefits flow to the individual who will bear some or all of the costs. However, the receiving university may benefit from the experience of teaching students from different academic backgrounds, and will gain or lose materially according to whether the fee received exceeds or falls short of the marginal teaching costs. In the case of doctoral students from abroad, published research work can bring academic credit to the receiving university and valuable links with rising scholars can be established.

From the point of view of the home nation, the return from postgraduates will in most cases be greater and enjoyed sooner than in the case of undergraduates, always assuming the postgraduates return to employment at home. The home country may lose, however, if the academic experience is inappropriate to its own social and economic needs. The result may be either the loss by brain drain or the inability to employ the returning student productively. The Third World has suffered a good deal, I believe, by sending many of their most promising postgraduates to universities in advanced countries to take courses which are either designed for quite different purposes or badly designed to serve Third World needs. Factors such as this can be crucial in assessing the value of sharing resources as a result of student or faculty mobility.

The provision of postgraduate-level courses in Third World universities, in part taught by faculty members on loan from universities in more advanced countries, has been more effective, more tuned to the needs and possibilities of Third World students, and could be developed further. In the UK, we have an organization, the Inter-Universities and Polytechnics Council, which finds staff to work on temporary assignment in Third World universities, and subsidizes the financial arrangements. I have learned from Professor Ørjar Øyen of an organization based in Yugoslavia which is concerned with organizing postgraduate-level teaching on an international basis. The transmission and reception of this information is a good example of the practical value of such gatherings as this symposium.

One mode of sharing facilities which has considerable advantages and attraction, but which appears remarkedly undeveloped, is joint ownership and management of an academic resource. It must be admitted that even within a small country there is much less of such sharing than would seem to be desirable. The anxiety to exercise unitary control (Is there such a thing, given the nature of university government?) appears to be strong, possibly strengthened by the desire to avoid even more complex structures of participatory democracy than occur within one university. In sharing between countries, the advantages (and the fascination effect) may outweigh the perceived problems. There are two cases which would seem to be worth exploration. The first case is where the costs are exceptionally high and there are benefits of wide interest and applicability: "Big science" provides obvious examples. It appears that governments find it easier to develop such sharing arrangements than do freestanding universities, perhaps because the latter attach too high a value to being freestanding. The second case is when the nature of the subject derives benefit from a sharing arrangement, e.g., in such fields as international relations, international trade, cross-cultural studies, anthropology, and so forth. There is great potential for fruitful sharing of resources, both for teaching and research.

Furthermore, in subjects of this sort, there is no need for a single location. (Clearly, location is the first issue to be resolved where the concentration of high-cost resources makes the case for sharing.) Great strength could be provided to the work of what otherwise would be small specialist units in single universities by above all, perhaps, a very flexible approach towards shared resources, a small common policy-making body meeting (say) twice a year, the full exchange of information, and the regular exchange of staff and of postgraduates. There would, of course, be costs, but the benefits could be much greater. The sharing of highly specialized teaching resources allied with the phasing of some teaching modules on (say) a two-year rather than on a one-year basis could achieve higher academic quality at lower cost than would have been possible on a "go it alone" basis. The gain both in specialism and in the intellectual stimuli provided by different approaches from different backgrounds suggest to me that more academic multinationalism should be encouraged, but achieved by merger rather than take-over or the establishment of out-stations by a metropolitan university.

Is it appropriate to take the case for international exchanges and other forms of sharing for granted? In Britain it has been found necessary to debate the case because of a mistaken decision by our government to substitute a confused mixture of market philosophy and government determination of minimum fees for a comprehensive policy. The advantages for the receiving country have been stated succinctly, as follows:

> ...strengthening and broadening our own education and research, promotion of intellectual and cultural contacts, influence with decision-makers in other countries, development of trade opportunities, income and employment for Britons from rendering educational services to overseas clients, making a constructive contribution to overseas development, a positive role in the world community. If overseas students themselves showed no particular inclination to study in this country, Britain would nevertheless have her own interest in inducing them to come.[3]

As you may know, these points have led our government to dilute its policy somewhat, mainly in relation to students from the Commonwealth, particularly Hong Kong, Malaysia, and Cyprus. The total of additional spending on support for overseas students will be at approximately 15 million pounds per annum, about half of which is new money, the other half being reallocated from the Aid Program. Perhaps of greatest interest -- and potential -- is the declaration by the British government that:

> Britain should be ready in principle to negotiate reciprocal fee concessions with countries receiving roughly as many British students as they send to her although the prospects for major agreements look somewhat remote. Government-to-government reciprocal concessions are not practicable since, for example, central government in Canada and the USA have

no responsibility for the level of tuition fees in educational establishments. However, there may be scope for some limited extensions of existing arrangements whereby institutions in this country negotiate reciprocal concessionary fee status directly with institutions overseas. The Government is ready to encourage this by considering proposals from institutions on ways of extending these arrangements.[4]

It is too early to say what opportunities may develop as a result of a recent statement from the British Foreign Office (February 1983). A key issue is whether there would be additional financial support to enable reciprocal exchanges with Third World countries for which the cost of fares and providing adequate pocket-money in Britain could be a deterrent. Such reciprocal exchanges between universities in advanced countries are easier to conclude, but even in these cases disparate costs can create difficulties.

The University of Stirling has operated exchange programs with North America since 1969. At present there are agreements with seven North American universities, one being the University of California. All of these have been reciprocal since 1979-1980. The schemes vary in detail. The general pattern, however, is for a reciprocal exchange of tuition, food, and accommodation costs. On the simplest model, the University of Stirling pays tuition, food, and accommodation for the American students, and the American university pays these items for the Stirling students. In the more complex schemes, food and tuition costs are not exchanged and the sending university and/or the overseas student pay these. In all cases vacation periods are excluded from the arrangements. American students coming to Stirling pay their own personal and travel expenses. The University of Stirling pays personal expenses for Stirling students sent to America, and these students pay trans-Atlantic travel and overseas medical insurance from their own resources.

At Stirling a fairly compact administrative structure operates to ensure that the academic and financial arrangements for exchange programs operate smoothly. The importance of effective administration cannot be stressed too strongly. The administration costs per capita are very heavy, quite apart from the current level of subsidy provided by the university (approximately $750 per student); however, these costs are, in our view, clearly outweighed by the benefits derived by our students who go to North America and the more widely shared benefits which the university and its campus life derive from having undergraduates from North America with us.

Very few established links have passed out of existence, e.g., in one case because the American university had a habit of removing courses at short notice, a practice which led us to withdraw. On the other hand, we have more requests to establish new reciprocal links than we can accept. It may be that the government policy statement already referred to will enable us to extend our range either through existing links or by establishing new ones. We are currently in discussion concerning the establishment of two additional North American links on a reciprocal basis.

In addition to these reciprocal links (which are in high demand and strongly competed for on both sides), Stirling has a number of informal links, with no reciprocity necessarily involved. There are four such arrangements with three universities in the United States. These arrangements commit the university to admit specified numbers of suitably qualified students from the American universities. Stirling also has links with five universities in Western Europe, one in Eastern Europe, and one in Malaysia. All of these are at the university level. There are, of course, many informal links at the departmental level which operate on the basis of personal contact and trust.

Many students from overseas come outside of any exchange scheme, reciprocal or otherwise. Indeed, the majority of foreign students come on an ad hoc basis, usually attracted by what they have been advised is a course which matches their needs. Most universities will have several specialist courses which have particular appeal, often to postgraduate students from abroad. At Stirling, for example, courses in aquaculture, accountancy, and bibliographical studies illustrate that point. Effective advertising and word-of-mouth recommendation usually means that such courses are substantially over-subscribed by well qualified candidates. Given this, it may seem surprising that quite generous bursary schemes are available to enable students to come from abroad. Again, illustrating from Stirling, we provide bursaries which can reduce the total cost of residence, maintenance, and tuition by between 25 to 50 percent according to the level of course and associated fees. The reason for this level of support from receiving universities is, I think, a mixture of a marginal cost pricing policy and the off-setting of short-run and long-run benefits for the university against the cost of the subsidy.

Academic communities do believe most strongly in the benefits of exchange, of mobility, of international links and are prepared to make sacrifices to encourage these desirable objectives. It has always been so. It is interesting that when arts students at Oxford were asked at the beginning of the seventeenth century if migration stimulates philosophical thinking, the students were required to give reasons why the answer was "yes" -- revealing, it should be said, a rather stunted form of philosophical thinking. There is certainly some evidence that some of the wandering scholars of medieval Europe, the gyrovagus as they have been styled, found the delights of travel for its own sake more than a counterbalance to scholarship pursuits. "It is a strange madness," said Petrarch, "this desire to be forever sleeping in a strange bed."[5] Scholarly exchanges on a more formalized basis may have kept the non-academic purposes of academic travel somewhat in check.

The third category of assets which can be shared -- research opportunities -- is the one most frequently overlooked. Every scholar concerned with comparative studies must seek some of the necessary research material abroad. Scholars in particular subjects may have to seek most of their research material abroad. While British historians specializing in early American history and in later Indian history may find some of the necessary raw material at home, much of it requires extended visits to the country being studied. Their interest may bring new approaches and new insights. If it is accepted that the detection of anomalies is a significant path to scientific advances, then in the arts and, in particular, the social sciences, a visiting "incomer" is more likely to detect anomalies than the established native, who has come to accept the framework as given. To the extent that this is so, the sharing of research resources can prove most fruitful to the self-understanding of the receiving country. By way of illustration, some of the most perceptive and influential work on the post-Second World War problems of the British economy have come from visiting scholars. In particular, I would suggest that the interaction between social attitudes and industrial relations is much more clearly perceived, explained, and to some extent improved, as a result of foreign scholarship than of the home-grown variety. This is not a function of the quality of different scholars, but of the value systems and general preconceptions which are attached to them. In this connection, it is appropriate to mention the outstanding contribution which Dr. Clark Kerr has made to the understanding, in Britain, of industrial relations[6] and the similarly valuable contribution Professor Dahrendorf has made by his analysis of Britain's economic and industrial problems.[7]

A related point concerns the exchange of resources across systems, particularly between the Communist Eastern bloc and the Western democracies. At Stirling we have a staff exchange arrangement with Katowice in Poland. The introduction of martial law gave rise to much debate and heart-searching at Stirling. Should the link be ostentatiously broken as a sign of support for Solidarity, or quietly continued as a sign of support for academics in Poland, numbers of whom had become known to us as a result of two-way visits? The university came down firmly for the second course, and there is evidence that this is what our academic friends in Poland prefer. Whereas within systems the extent of debate with subject areas varies according to circumstances, it is probably true that the humanities are a unifying factor between scholars of different nations which broadly share the same value systems. The opposite holds in cross-system exchanges. The visiting political theorist who assumes or even propagates the concept of liberal democracy in an East European university will more likely break a link rather than forge one. Similarly, though the reasons may be different, the reception given in the West to a political scientist from Eastern Europe who cannot criticize weaknesses in the Leninist state will also probably reduce the enthusiasm for exchange rather than enhance it. Yet these are the exchanges which are most needed and which could prove most fruitful. Much patient and sensitive work is required on both sides if such exchanges are to be fostered, and this must be done in the first instance because both sides believe that they can learn from each other. Operated for different motives -- the motives of diplomacy rather than of scholarship -- such links would prove damaging to the universities at each end of the link.

Informal, person-to-person sharing arrangements are widespread in the international academic world. It is an unfortunate academic who is not a "member" of at least one network built up in this way.

Such networks can work effectively only if the universities in which their members function help them to work, or if research councils and like bodies see virtue in providing support in the form of travel and maintenance costs. The availability of sabbatical leave is clearly of great importance, but requires financial support to turn that into opportunities to teach or to carry on research abroad. The unfortunate tendency for academic salaries to fall behind prices and costs, accentuated by greater instability in foreign currency exchanges, has had the effect of reducing the "spare" resources available to encourage travel abroad, particularly on sabbatical leave. This effect again throws the problem back to the institutional level, although the links may be informal.

In the UK, the British Council administers an Academic Trust Grant Scheme which provides the finances to promote direct contact between departments and institutions with medical, scientific, or academic interests and to encourage the development of longer term collaboration and research. About sixty academics from Scotland's eight universities have made visits under this scheme over the last twelve months. The figure by no means covers all of such academic visits. University funds send many more and we are fortunate in Scotland to have additional funding available from the Carnegie Trust for the universities of Scotland. My very approximate estimate is that 5 percent of academic faculty go abroad in any one year, a good figure but probably still not maximizing the potential benefits of exchange.

In order to secure the widest possible sharing of academic talent and resources, and to close in on the potential that we know very well is not being fully realized, do we need new institutional arrangements or only more of the kind we already have? Indeed, do we, perhaps, need new institutions capable of developing new arrangements? Already we have a United Nations University (UNU) and a university sponsored by the member countries of the EEC. In Europe a move is afoot to give existing national centers of excellence a European designation and role. The research projects of UNU are beginning to attract some attention from within national universities. It is to be hoped that such continental and international universities develop more as links and facilitators of international cooperation than as independent stand-alone institutions staffed on the basis of national quotas.

So much of the genuinely international in world scholarship is ad hoc, even accidental, and so much of that is dependent in the first instance on external (to the academic scene) initiative and funding, that a place must be found to stimulate internationalism in scholarship for the sake of scholarship, and in a more coordinated and far-sighted way.

Dr. Graham Hills, principal and vice chancellor of the University of Strathclyde -- one of the three leading technological universities in the UK -- returned from a visit to the United States with the concept of "circles of quality meetings," bringing together either five or ten leading specialists from the United States and Scotland to review the present position of their specialism and discuss areas of new research, possibly resulting in partnership or integrated programs. The concept is an exciting one, though realism and modesty require me to say that one-for-one matching of talent, Scotland to the United States, may be rather difficult to achieve in some specialist fields. However, Dr. Hills has, I understand, received some financial backing for the concept and we are both hopeful that this idea can be carried into practice. One source of help, and often initiative, comes from international industry, the multinationals. In The Age of Discontinuity, Professor Peter Drucker observes:

> There is an...institution that the world economy needs; a producing and distributing institution that is not purely national in its economic operations and point of view. The world economy needs someone who represents its interests against all the partial and particular interests of its various members....Traditionally such an institution has always been political, that is, a government. Because the world economy is strictly an economic community the institution that represents it will have to be an economic rather than a political institution. Indeed it cannot possibly function unless it respects the political institutions of the national state. The individual sovereign states, especially the big strong developed countries, will not accept a super government of any kind. Such an institution...we already have at hand. Its development during the last twenty years may well be the most significant event in the world economy and the one that, in the long run, will bring the greatest benefits. The institution is the 'multinational corporation'. [8]

Is there a resource here which the academic world ought to try to develop more systematically? Are some of the great talents employed in MNEs available as participants in the organization and functioning of scholarly work at an international level? I can imagine the horror with which some academics would regard such a suggestion -- and I do so accepting that the fears expressed would not be without foundation. But, would conscious and coordinated cooperation not be better than the present ad hoc arrangements in which there is very considerable interaction between multinational companies and single, nationally based universities, but no organizational response on the academic side of the international level?

There was a suggestion (Ed. note: Chapter 7) that some linkages between the universities at an international level might establish a "sixth continent." But the multinational corporations arrived there first; if there is a sixth continent, they are it. The question is: How are we going to deal with them? How are we going to make them play their part in scholarship?

I began with one North American sceptic, Mark Twain; let me close with another, that ornament of his age and of this nation, Benjamin Franklin. On the second of August 1776, he said, "We must indeed all hang together, or most assuredly, we shall all hang separately." [9] Is that not the best reason there could be for the free-minded academics of the world to hang together, sharing the resources of their trade as far as it is compatible with their responsibility to the young of their own country?

If we want to do more than lay a foundation on which a more expansive future can be built, we have to develop the case, find the means, and strengthen the institutions which are required to ensure this.

NOTES

1. Mark Twain, Sketches New and Old, 1900, p.350.

2. John H. Horlock, Speech at Open University, February 1, 1983.

3. Overseas Students' Trust, A Policy for Overseas Students (London: 1982), p.70.

4. Statement by British Foreign and Commonwealth Secretary in House of Commons, February 8, 1983, Official Report, Vol. 36.

5. Helen Waddell, The Wandering Scholars (London: Constable, 1942), p.161.

6. Clark Kerr and A. Siegal, "The Inter-Industry Propensity to Strike - An International Comparison," in A. Kornhauser et al, Industrial Conflict (New York: McGraw Hill, 1954) and Clark Kerr et al, Industrialism and Industrial Man (Cambridge, MA: Harvard University Press, 1960).

7. Ralf Dahrendorf (ed.), Europe's Economy in Crisis (London: Weidenfeld and Nicolson, 1982).

8. Peter Drucker, The Age of Discontinuity (London: Wm. Heinemann, Ltd., 1969), p.93.

9. Benjamin Franklin, Remark to John Hancock at the signing of the Declaration of Independence. See p.286 in Ronald W. Clark, Benjamin Franklin, A Biography (New York: Random House, 1983).

11
Beyond Scholarship

R. J. Snow

My experience in international education, particularly in connection with the Education Abroad Program, has been similar to that described by many of the contributors to this volume who have been directors, or who have had other kinds of administrative experience in international exchange. It was, I think, the most stimulating two-year period of my professional life, and it certainly was reorienting in terms of my whole approach to higher education. It has been extremely useful.

I think the last two papers complement each other very nicely. Vice Chancellor Svenson (Ed. note: Chapter 9) gave us the dynamic which he thinks underlies international exchange in higher education. But, I find it mildly disquieting to have his definition of scholarship so simply, starkly, and clearly expressed as "the scholar himself serving his own self-interests," and then to have "scholarship" alone be the basic measure of the utility of exchange programs. It is disquieting because so much more seemed to be happening during my personal experience abroad, especially with regard to undergraduate education. I thought the impact of international exchange in Bordeaux beyond strict scholarship was very visible. The University of Bordeaux itself was quite different because our students were there. The <u>community</u> around the university was different, and better, because of <u>the</u> exchange. And so, when so much more occurs than "scholarship," I find the Svenson description too constraining.

Fundamentally, however, I think it is hard to take issue with the notion that all exchange must be based on productive scholarly activity and, in fact, this idea feeds Svenson's later analysis of the guidelines we ought to use to evaluate whether we continue international exchange programs or not. If academic work of proper quality is <u>not</u> resulting from what we are doing, then clearly it should not be pursued.

I think Sir Kenneth's paper (Ed. note: Chapter 10) provides a nice array of resources which can be shared. From the perspective of an administrator away from international exchange for a time, and eager to stimulate such exchange on my own campus, I found the fundamental goal of "sharing academic resources" to be helpful as a planning concept. This concept seems superior to the more narrowly focused goals of assuring faculty a productive academic experience, or of providing a research-oriented graduate student with the specific support needed to find the cubbyholes and archives in order to complete a focused piece of research, or, for that matter, of focusing only on what is needed at minimum for a useful undergraduate student exchange.

If one starts with a notion of an array of academic resources to be shared, one is led to ask questions which one might otherwise not ask about facilities, programs, and other resources. For example, it is interesting to learn about the exchange between the University of Stirling physics program students and the University of California. This new initiative grows out of a focus on sharing.

From such a focus, one might ask additional questions about the case studies reported by Vice Chancellor Svenson. Might there not have been the possibility of integrating some undergraduate programs in connection with the graduate research emphasis which seemed to be primary in his focus? Obviously, faculty resources are of prime importance in sharing. Faculty must ultimately define programs and administer them in consonance with proper academic values. But where a program already has senior faculty or even advance graduate students in place to provide undergraduate advisory and supervisory tasks, even while advancing their own causes, it may be possible to introduce some undergraduate experience there as well.

Finally, it seems to me that one category not explicitly treated by Sir Kenneth is the benefit to be derived from the interaction of administrative staff in international exchange. I participated in the Education Abroad Program at Bordeaux a decade ago and have been aware of the evolution of that center ever since. It is quite clear that the University of Bordeaux is not the same place as it was before. Its administrative staff and faculty think and relate differently than they did in the early years of the program, both between themselves and with California faculty. For the most part, this evolution has been a happy one. Most of its positive aspects can be traced to this university, and to the care that California administrators have taken with Bordeaux counterparts, as well as to the experience gained from linkages which those in Bordeaux have had with other universities with exchange programs on their campus as well.

It is certainly clear that the last twenty years of EAP at the University of California have resulted in an evolution in this institution which, in my view, makes it the leader in international education, especially with regard to undergraduate programs. So, I would add the very productive, evolutionary, and stimulating effect of administrative interchange to the faculty, student, and facilities resources mentioned, and to the special research opportunities to which Sir Kenneth has alluded.

Part Five

Epilogue

12 Report of the Symposium Rapporteur

Naftaly G. Glasman

This summary statement is based on remarks I prepared for the dinner meeting which closed the EAP Symposium on International Education. I have since expanded on my original presentation, however, to include some material and comments by some of the sectional rapporteurs and chairpersons.

The International Character of Higher Education

Although in its early years higher education crossed national boundaries and represented intellectual borrowing on a large scale, forces developed which have made it less international. These include the nation-state's utilization of higher education as an instrument of power; the nationalization of higher education; the multiplicity of languages of instruction; and the closing of doors to students from other countries.

In my opinion, the reason for the centrality of higher education in the world is that higher education is by definition international, even though the gulf which separates nations is wide. Politicians sometimes tell us otherwise in their rhetoric. In fact, when leaders of rival nations meet, their joint statements to the press always include a paragraph which represents a consensus of their rival positions. The problem with such statements is that they are so general in nature that they can be interpreted in a million and one ways. Those of us who teach a little bit of political science know that the only way to achieve consensus in rhetoric between opposing parties is to phrase the rhetoric as abstractly as possible, so that it appears to reflect agreement. This enables each side to interpret the language in a way which suits its purpose.

But the gulf between nations is wide nonetheless. Let me illustrate how wide it is with just one example. A secret meeting took place recently. Prime Minister Begin visited President Reagan and saw three telephones on his desk, a red one, a white one, and a blue one. He asked, "Mr. President, what is the red phone for?"

The President replied, "Oh, that is to call the secretary of defense."

"What is the white phone for?"

"Oh, that is to call the chairman of the Joint Chiefs of Staff."

"What is the blue one for?"

"Oh, to call God."

"May I speak with Him?"

"Sure."

Begin dials the number, speaks to God, hangs up, and says, "Thank you, Mr. President. How much is it going to be?"

"Well, the cost will be $35." The prime minister writes out a check for this amount.

A month later, in the prime minister's office, the president notices three telephones on the prime minister's desk, a red one, a white one, and a blue one. The president asks, "What is the red phone for?"

"Oh, that is to call the minister of defense."

"What is the white phone for?"

"Oh, that is to call the chief of staff."

"What is the blue phone for?"

"Oh, that is to call God."

"May I speak with Him?"

"Certainly."

President Reagan dials the number, speaks with God, hangs up, and says, "Thank you, Mr. Prime Minister. What will it cost?"

"Oh, nothing. Here it is a local call."

The question is: How can international higher education help close the gaps? I don't think anyone expects higher education to do the entire job.

In addition to the papers which were presented and are contained in this volume, chairmen and rapporteurs of the discussion sessions provided additional insights and helpful summaries of their group discussions which bear upon the role that higher education can play in closing those gaps.

Self-Evident Nature of the International Character of Higher Education

Professor David Messick noted how the internationality of higher education is so self-evident that it is often overlooked. He illustrated this by referring to a course he was teaching:

> It is a course entitled, "Cooperation, Competition and Conflict." One of the texts that I have assigned in this course is a book entitled, The Science of Conflict by a sociologist, James Schellenberg. The third chapter of the book begins with a discussion of Darwin's work. He, of course, was British. The fourth chapter discusses Karl Marx's ideas. Marx was German. In the same chapter, some of Professor Dahrendorf's ideas are discussed. So, seventy-some students here at UCSB will be studying some of Professor Dahrendorf's ideas on social conflict, and this will happen with no hoopla or ceremony. This is the kind of international education that occurs every day, unmarked and unnoticed, because it is simply part of what all of us do, day in and day out, in a university.

The Undergraduate Dimension

Professor Howard Shuman summarized major points in the discussion which dealt with undergraduate study abroad:

> That higher education is international is not sufficiently noticed. The debate between the British and the American versus the continental European traditions was highlighted: the former being to provide specialized training and the latter to engender international sophistication The two traditions suggest different solutions. The values recognized by exchange students include the nature of the family, the centrality of the locality, and the role of government in politics.

The University in the Third World

Professor Murray Thomas provided this summary:

> The population of the Third World encompasses 75 percent of the world population. Furthermore, 75 percent of the foreign students in the United States are from the Third World. Yet, only 5 percent of American students and professors go to the Third World. Closing boundaries between nations is dangerous. American students who do go should be prepared to adapt. Higher education relationships between the Third World and industrial nations help both sides if they are a function of the identity of each.

Dr. Charles McCormack offered these comments:

> The university of the Third World has country-specific roles growing out of the unique economic and cultural conditions of their nations and regions, on the one hand, and common relations with the university and higher education community worldwide, on the other. Having spent all of my overseas academic career teaching and learning in Third World universities, representing the Experiment in International Living and the School for International Training, the majority of whose undergraduate students are involved with Third World programs, it is clear to me how much we in this country have to learn from the approaches, disciplines, and content of Third World educational institutions.

Academic and Cultural Dimensions of Study Abroad

Personal Aspects of the Study Abroad Experience

Two models were presented. Features of the personal growth model included the disruptive nature of the experience; the development of new ways of thinking, even in the hard sciences; acquiring of new ways of social interaction while at the same time experiencing feelings of separation and of ambivalence towards both countries. The second model was that of social diffusion. Various goals of exchange programs were enumerated. A dominant theme seemed to be the ambiguity of goals. The term "marginals" (cultural relativists) versus the term "centrals" (ethnocentrists) was introduced. A beautiful concept was introduced: "the strength of weak ties."

Professor Messick provided these additional thoughts:

> We tend to have two purposes for sending students abroad: one is to provide specialized academic training, and the other is to provide the much more vague, but, perhaps, more important characteristics that we associate with an educated person, i.e., the qualities of sophistication, civilization, breadth of knowledge, wisdom, judiciousness, tolerance, and other qualities. We need to think about the relative importance of these goals and what factors interfere with their achievement.

Professor Robert Billigmeier, from his years of experience in international education, made this observation:

> I think one of the disturbing things about the experience of most young people abroad is that they are so readily impressed with what they have learned. It is, after all, so much more than they knew before. They often are quite quickly persuaded that they have mastered far more than they actually have, that they have explored far more than, in reality, they have done. This amiable self-deception may bring frustration and disillusionment.

Foreign Language and Culture

The discussion on foreign language and culture was summarized by Professor Elijah Lovejoy. His report gave much more attention to language than to culture. In the area of language, foreign experience seemed to be better than learning another language through drills. But, some speakers said that that experience was a shallow one. Obstacles that were enumerated included the self-sufficiency of the American society, poor language teaching, and the emphasis on science and technology.

There was a call for a two-tier program in the Education Abroad Program for language teaching: one for beginners and one for advanced students. Language was described as a house, a place in which to survive. It was noted that the military and some private industrial firms have the best language schools. Only two major statements concerning culture were noted. One was the need to overcome prejudice; the other was the need for a depth approach as far as possible.

Disciplinary Points of View

Humanities: In summarizing major points covered in this group, Professor Jerry Carlson reported as follows:

> Basic questions were posed. Is exchange really possible? Is it only for elitists? Access to foreign culture through foreign language was recommended. Literature related to national and historical dimensions was emphasized. Science students can benefit from what is studied in the humanities in the foreign culture. It was noted that the

number of students in computer science and engineering has increased recently while the number of students in the physical sciences has remained about the same. In the humanities the number has decreased. Cross-cultural, trans-discipline experience is called for if students are to be educated.

Social Sciences: Professor Howard Clarke summarized the discussion group which dealt with the social sciences:

Even though social science students who study abroad learn to know what it is like to live meaningfully in another society, some disadvantages were noted: political bias in some university departments, as well as excessive technicalities and strict policies in others. This session called for cross-disciplinary types of academic experiences and also raised the issue of graduate students rather than undergraduates. The involvement of American students in local partisan politics was debated.

International and Comparative Studies: This session was summarized by Professor William Dukes. This was a "heavy one," even for people in the social and behavioral sciences. The internationalism of science was the focus. It can be facilitated through a deeper understanding of the object of interest, possibly more than taking additional courses in foreign languages or in international relations. Scientists operate so as to preserve the international orientation. Comparative methods in the social sciences are similar to inquiry methods in the physical sciences. Yet, there is a bent towards parochialism in some social and behavioral science disciplines.

Would you believe that someone in this session suggested that one example of a discipline that shows parochialism is higher education? What would the next president of the university say to us if he heard such an allegation? Internationalism is both "worldwide" and "between nations." In querying Professor Dukes as to what this meant, I was told that "worldwide" reflects a community of scholars and "between nations" reflects cultural exchange. Someone in the session also suggested that graduate schools promote international education. I happen to believe in that wholeheartedly.

Science and Technology: Dr. Henry Weaver, at the beginning of the session, introduced the topic in this way:

When I was a graduate student, the late William Mosher sat down with us one day in the Chemistry Department and talked about the differences in the approach to chemistry in the United Kingdom and in the United States. He pointed out that the discovery of penicillin probably could not have taken place in America. Had Fleming been an American scientist and discovered a mold killing his bacteria, he would have thrown a little copper sulfate or something in order to kill the mold and proceeded with the original experiment, rather than asking the question, "Why is that mold killing it?" and then, departing from the initial purpose of the experiment, searching for the answer to the new question.

I think that often we tend to say that science and mathematics are the same in any country and that, therefore, in principle, a student in those fields would not go abroad for academic reasons. However, it would be assumed that the location would be relevant in a few cases: for example, geology, marine biology, or if a student is dealing with different flora and fauna. Again, it is assumed that there is no academic reason to go abroad in electrical engineering, but there might be reason for plant physiology majors to do so because the plants are different.

Thus, the question must be raised: Are there academic reasons for undergraduates to be educated abroad in science and technology, or do the reasons stem primarily from the fact that scientists and technologists cross more national boundaries in their research and travel and thus must develop more cross-cultural sensitivity than those in other disciplines?

Professor Adil Yaqub summarized the science and technology session:

It is a small world and it is getting smaller, but the issue is: When should students go? As undergraduates? As graduate students? Postdoctorates? Major issues mentioned included language barriers for foreign students in the United States, the lack of electives for some science, computer, and engineering students, and the length of the foreign stay. There was general agreement that the study of science and the exchange of science students could be important factors in preserving peace.

Sharing Academic Resources: The Ultimate Potential of University Linkage

The speakers were extremely exciting and the views behind them were even more so. One question was: What are the resources themselves? Institutions? Individual faculty and students? Research? Other questions were: Why share? and, how to share? Particular university needs were mentioned, such as scholarships and covering the costs of international involvement. It was suggested that sharing ought to be based on academic merit and on viability. Political factors were mentioned as sometimes being more crucial than others in the sharing of academic resources.

At this symposium, not only were we international, but we were interpersonal. Perhaps, in the final analysis, the key to the intensification of the former is the fortification of the latter.

13 The Kind of Education Demanded by Today's World

David S. Saxon

These papers, which were presented in connection with the 115th anniversary chartering of the University of California and the symposium marking the 20th anniversary of the University's Education Abroad Program, have been devoted to the theme of international education and what it means to universities like our own and those abroad, what the potentialities for various disciplines are, and how we can strengthen the ties that bind us through international exchange.

The scope and variety of the topics are quite remarkable and interesting. I suppose that most of those visiting from abroad thought that such an anniversary as the twentieth was a youthful one. But in this country we think of it as indicating maturity and even a degree of venerability.

I am especially pleased that the theme of the Charter Day, my last as President of the University, is international education. I have been thinking over the past two or three years quite a bit about the question of education, about what it means to be a liberally educated person in today's world. I will oversimplify by describing that world as one which is dominated by three characteristics: it is technological; it is xenophobic; and it is nuclear. I have come to several conclusions about the kind of education such a world demands, conclusions that are neither original nor even very new. But the very fact that they are neither original nor new means that we are dealing with problems that are difficult and not very easily translated into action.

The first of my conclusions is that we must give students an education that makes it possible for them to understand that the sciences and the humanities are intimately related at the deepest level because they are complementary responses to mankind's deepest needs. Let me quote from Gerald Holton, Professor of Physics at Harvard University, who delivered the 1981 Jefferson Lectures. In his remarks, Professor Holton refers to a 1964 report from the Commission on Humanities, a report that was the first step towards the establishment of the National Endowment for the Humanities. The Commission made clear in its report that it considers that:

> ....science, as a technique and expression of intellect, is in fact closely affiliated with the humanities....the natural

> sciences, the social sciences, and the humanities are by their very nature, allies....if the interdependence of science and the humanities were more generally understood, men would be more likely to become masters of their technology, and not its unthinking servants.[1]

My second conclusion, which follows from the first, is that all students, nonscientists and scientists, must understand in today's technological, xenophobic, and nuclear world both the character and the limits to science. Let me again cite from Professor Holton's speech, this time a remark he quotes from the first Jefferson Lecture, which was given by Lionel Trilling in 1972:

> The old humanistic faith conceived science, together with mathematics, to be almost as readily accessible to understanding and interest as literature and history....[but] physical science lies beyond the intellectual grasp of most men....its operative conceptions are alien to the mass of educated persons....they do not engage emotion or challenge imagination....this exclusion of most of us from the mode of thought which is habitually said to be the characteristic achievement of the modern age....introduces into the life of the mind a significant element of dubiety and alienation....[2]

There are reasons for Trilling's feeling about the difficulty of understanding science and the difficulty of accepting the notion that science is accessible, not inaccessible. One reason is that modern science deals with the aspects of nature that are remote from our daily experience. I once read somewhere a paper written by Lord Rayleigh in the late nineteenth century or early twentieth century which begins with the remark that he was out walking past a pond and noticed on the surface of the pond not only waves but ripples. He said that he began to wonder about the difference between those two phenomena. He then went on to provide a theory of ripples, which have a different physical origin than waves. It would be very difficult to find a paper in physics today which starts out with that kind of homely, direct observation.

We <u>are</u> dealing with matters which are infinitely remote, in a certain sense, from our daily experience. Furthermore, unfortunately, most of our population is not even in a position to draw a set of satisfactory conclusions about its own experiences. I submit that in this world, in these times, no person can be called educated unless he understands the character and limits of science.

My third conclusion is that our scientists and engineers must understand the importance of other kinds of knowledge than scientific and technical, and other kinds of truths and understandings and values than those which can be observed and measured in the laboratory. In a technological, xenophobic, and nuclear world we simply cannot afford to depend for guidance on those who are merely technocrats, on those who are too narrowly educated, on those who are simply experts and nothing more. We must insist on wisdom and not merely knowledge from those who are and who will be leading us.

My last conclusion, one I emphasized in my remarks at the Charter Day ceremony, is that in this technological, xenophobic, and nuclear world, an understanding of other cultures is an indispensable attainment for anyone who aspires to be liberally educated. To some extent, it always has been. But now it is more important than ever, when technology has simultaneously linked us all closer together and vastly increased our capacity for mutual destruction.

One of the benefits of the universities is that they are among the few institutions in any society actively and constantly seeking to diminish the barriers that divide us from each other. They do that in a variety of ways. One way is through the establishment of international studies programs, which give students the chance to learn about the politics, history, and culture of other countries from an academic perspective. Another way is through the international exchange of students and faculty. This, of course, gives a much more immediate and first hand experience of the world from the perspective of other cultures and other countries. Both of these are essential and complementary elements of international studies, and at the University of California we are proud of the efforts we have made to give students both kinds of opportunities.

What I am arguing, and here I am qualified to speak only about American education, is that we need to do more. We need to make an understanding of other languages and other cultures an integral part of our undergraduate curriculum. We need to begin, indeed, to teach foreign languages in grade school, so that all of our students -- not just those who go on to a college or university -- will have the chance to acquire the skill in languages that is an essential prerequisite to a true understanding of another culture.

We need to instill in our students a sense of the great importance of such studies to their future, not only as a source of personal satisfaction, but as a way of preparing themselves to be citizens in a world that is becoming smaller and more precariously balanced all the time.

When you think about the values implicit in the commitment to international education -- an openness to other points of view, a broad perspective on the world, an appreciation of the richness and variety of experience -- it is clear that we could do worse than choose such an educational ideal both for our students and for ourselves.

NOTES

1. Report by the Commission on the Humanities, sponsored by the American Council of Learned Societies, Council of Graduate Schools in the United States, and United Chapters of Phi Beta Kappa (New York: 1964).

2. Lionel Trilling, Mind in the Modern World (Viking Press, 1973), pp.13-14.

Appendix

Symposium on Education Abroad
on the occasion of the University of California
115th Charter Anniversary
and
20th Anniversary of the Education Abroad Program

Santa Barbara, California
April 14-15, 1983

April 14, 2:00 p.m.: Charter Anniversary Ceremonies on the Faculty Club lawn. Presiding - David S. Saxon; Main speaker - Ralf Dahrendorf.

April 15, 9:00 a.m. - 10:00 p.m.: EAP Symposium on International Education.

There were three plenary sessions, the first two of which were followed by discussion groups. The symposium concluded with a reception and dinner at the Santa Barbara Inn. EAP Director William H. Allaway presided. Naftaly S. Glasman, the symposium rapporteur, summarized the sessions and discussions. David S. Saxon delivered the closing address.

In addition to the plenary speakers and discussants whose papers appear in this volume, other program participants are listed below.

Plenary Chairpersons:

Vernon I. Cheadle, Chancellor Emeritus and Professor of Botany Emeritus, UC Santa Barbara;

William B. Fretter, Vice President of the University of California Emeritus and Professor of Physics Emeritus, UC Berkeley;

Robert A. Huttenback, Chancellor and Professor of History, UC Santa Barbara.

Discussion Leaders:

Robert M. Billigmeier, Professor of Sociology, UC Santa Barbara and former Associate Director of the Education Abroad Program;

Sanford S. Elberg, Professor Emeritus, Biomedical and Environmental Health Sciences, Dean Emeritus of the Graduate Division, UC Berkeley and former Associate Director for Academic Affairs of the Education Abroad Program;

Homer Higbee, Assistant Dean of International Studies and Programs, Michigan State University;

Kibbey M. Horne, Director of International Programs, California State University;

Charles F. McCormack, President of the Experiment in International Living, Vermont and 2nd Chairman of the Consortium for International Citizen Exchange;

Arthur E. McGuinness, Professor of English, UC Davis and former Associate Director of the Education Abroad Program London office;

David M. Messick, Professor and Chair of Psychology, UC Santa Barbara and former Director of the Education Abroad Program Study Center at the University of Bergen;

Hideyasu Nakagawa, President of the International Christian University, Tokyo from 1975 to 1983;

Henry D. Weaver, Deputy Director of the Education Abroad Program and Adjunct Lecturer in Chemistry, UC Santa Barbara.

Rapporteurs:

Jerry S. Carlson, Professor of Education, UC Riverside, former Associate Director of the Education Abroad Program Study Center at Georg-August University, Goettingen and currently the Education Abroad Program's Coordinator for Research;

Howard W. Clarke, Chairman and Professor of Comparative Literature, UC Santa Barbara and former Associate Director and Director of the Education Abroad Program Study Center at Georg-August University, Goettingen;

William F. Dukes, Associate Director for Faculty Affairs of the Education Abroad Program, Professor of Psychology Emeritus, UC Davis and former Associate Director and Director of the Education Abroad Program Study Center at The Chinese University of Hong Kong;

Elijah P. Lovejoy, Associate Professor of Psychology, UC Santa Barbara and former Associate Director of the Education Abroad Program Study Center at The Chinese University of Hong Kong;

Birger A. Pearson, Professor of Religious Studies, UC Santa Barbara, former Associate Director for Academic Affairs of the Education Abroad Program and Director of the Education Abroad Program Study Center at the University of Lund;

Howard Shuman, 1983-1984 Senior Visiting Lecturer in Political Science, UC Santa Barbara;

R. Murray Thomas, Professor and Program Leader in International Education, UC Santa Barbara;

Adil Yaqub, Professor of Mathematics and the Campus Faculty Coordinator of the Education Abroad Program, UC Santa Barbara.

Index